# The Universal Language of Love

## Assessing Relationships through the Science of Emotional Availability

# The Universal Language of Love

## Assessing Relationships through the Science of Emotional Availability

Using more than 20 years of scientific research on emotional availability to understand human relationships:

- Caregiver-child
- Peer-peer
- Adult-adult
- Leaders

Zeynep Biringen, Ph.D.
Licensed Clinical Psychologist, State of Colorado
Professor and Director of Family & Developmental Studies (FDS)
    Graduate Program
    Department of Human Development & Family Studies
    Colorado State University

www.emotionalavailability.com;

## The Universal Language of Love
## Assessing Relationships through the Science of
## Emotional Availability

ISBN: 978-0-98-21303-0-08

Printed in the United States of America

Front Cover Design by Rebecca Finkel
Emotional Availability logos developed by Anthony Teneralli
(www.anthonyteneralli.com)

emotionalavailability.com
P.O. Box 3625
Boulder, CO 80307

www.emotionalavailability.com

# Dedication

This book is based on 20 years of scientific research on the concept of Emotional Availability (EA) conducted by me and my colleagues, first at the University of California at Berkeley while I was a doctoral student working with Dr. Mary Main, and later at the University of Colorado Health Science Center as a MacArthur Postdoctoral Fellow working with Drs. Robert Emde, Inge Bretherton, and Joseph Campos. I am indebted to Dr. Emde for his continued interest, inspiration, enthusiasm, and support in this area, and most of all for his creative spark on the topic of emotional expressions and emotional exchange, which has helped me to remain focused on this area. I also thank my colleagues in Australia, New Zealand, Germany, Israel, Belgium, The Netherlands, Italy, Korea, Peru, Brazil, Scotland, England, China, Japan, Portugal, Finland, Latvia, Turkey, Greece, Sweden, Norway, and my colleagues at numerous scientific laboratories in the United States who investigate U.S. subcultures, including (but not limited to) Colorado State University, Tufts University, The Pennsylvania State University, and the National Institutes of Health. I also thank my funders, including the National Science Foundation, the MacArthur Foundation, the U.S. Department of Defense, the Temple Hoyne Buell Foundation, and the Bohemian Foundation for work on Emotional Availability. The following academic journals featured special issues, for which I am grateful: *Attachment and Human Development, Infant Mental Health Journal, Journal of Early Childhood and Infant Psychology,* and *Parenting: Science and Practice.*

I thank wholeheartedly my husband of 31 years and our 15-year-old daughter for "being there" and the chance to apply the universal language of love.

I also thank Sandra Rush who provided editing expertise, feedback, and numerous ideas throughout the writing process.

This book is especially dedicated to all the children, families, and leaders (those who work with children in our communities, such as child care directors, providers, attorneys, and medical professionals) who helped me jumpstart this area of work on relationships and its impact on other relationships.

# Preface

In this book, I present an understanding of a simple, yet profound view of love in relationships. It is about real love and how it is expressed, as uncovered by researchers and clinicians in more than 20 years of scientific research and clinical practice on emotional availability (EA). This work has been conducted in the United States and by international investigators in more than 20 countries around the world. Here, I describe the principles revealed by the research and give you a chance to test your own relationships.

Although the stories of patients and research participants presented in this book are real (e.g., from my own work or the national or international work for which I consulted or my direct observations), critical information about individuals is changed and/or masked to maintain confidentiality. The gender, names, occupations, and any other potentially identifying information are fictional.

# Table of Contents

Explores the emotional availability of leaders who work with children (e.g., child care professionals, child care directors), those who have a say-so related to children (e.g., judges, attorneys), and political leaders (e.g., US or international lawmakers).

Helps in understanding how the psychological health of early as well as current attachment relationships frees us to become emotionally available people, including emotionally available leaders. The extent of EA in an individual depends on that individual's past as well as present experiences with attachment figures as well as the dedicated "reworking" of these experiences with attachment figures.

# 1 The Universal Language of Love: Emotional Availability and Unavailability

Emotional availability (EA) is a captivating, complex, and also a simple idea that describes how we can and should all relate to others, particularly those we value. EA is also about how we hope to be treated by those who value us. Simply put, it is the "universal language of love," uncovered by scientific research about relationships. The scientific work for the most part has centered on parent-child relationships (with the child age ranging between 0 and 14 years), but this concept of relationships is universal in the sense that it applies to many different types of relationships that matter. Further, EA has been found to be profoundly descriptive of what is considered of value in all the cultures in which it has been implemented, numbering more than 20 cultures around the globe.

Several years ago, Daniel Goleman wrote a book, *Emotional Intelligence*, which became a national bestseller. In it, he described the importance of emotional intelligence (defined as a combination of emotional and interpersonal skills) when it came to predicting success and happiness in life. More important, he advocated that emotional intelligence could and should be taught, including to the next generation. Emotional availability, as the universal language of love, is similar in many ways to the idea of emotional intelligence with certain distinctions: (1) EA is uniquely focused on individual and specific relationships, rather than on an overall outlook or trait, meaning that someone may be emotionally available in one relationship but not in another; (2) EA can be applied to a wide array of relationships, beginning with the newborn period but also including all ages of adults in relationships with others; and (3) EA is based on scientific evidence of the last 20 years.

Luckily, science and research have lent individuals a hand by studying the emotional needs of babies, children, parents, and other adults, and the dynamics of relationships. I have been fortunate to be a part of this

1

wave of scientific interest in relationships. For over 20 years, my work has focused on exploring how parents and children connect emotionally. As a doctoral candidate in child psychology at the University of California at Berkeley in 1987, I began to develop an assessment tool called the Emotional Availability Scales, to be described later in the book. This simple measurement, now used in clinics and research studies around the world, is an extremely accurate calibration of the quality and quantity of emotional connection between parents and children.

In my own research, as well as that of my colleagues, the emotional quality of parental relationships with children is of paramount importance. How parents talk to or hold an infant, the tone of their voices, the way they feed the child—all teach children more about emotional connection than anything else anyone could do, say, or teach directly. Further, this instrument has been used in measuring different types of relationships: newborn baby-mother, older baby-mother, child-father, child-child care professional, therapist-patient, peer-peer, and so on. I expect it to be of paramount importance in understanding all types of relationships, including adult-adult relationships and in terms of leaders' relationships with others.

Emotional availability is considered to be a universal language of love because it has been found to be used in more than 20 different cultures— subcultures in the United States as well as different countries—including but not limited to those in North America, South America, Europe, Asia, Australia, and New Zealand, with plans for studies in other continents. These scientific projects have been mainly focused on mothers and children and have documented that relationships with higher EA predict better outcomes for children. Psychiatrists also have found that a higher EA in the therapist-client relationship is indicative of more improvement in functioning for the client. What these findings suggest is that although we are separated by some of our differences, one thing—emotional connection—is definingly important in all cultures studied and is a predictor of good outcomes. I refer to EA as the universal language of love because it is the feeling of an emotional connection that is most crucial for relationships and that seems to bode well for those in all the cultures studied.

But, what does an emotional connection really mean? Does it mean liking each other? Loving each other? Being crazy about each other?

From the science of emotional availability, an emotional connection refers to just the *right amount and quality* of emotional connection, not merely the amount of a feeling. I might be totally in love with my baby, but if I cannot let her out of my sight, even when she is two years old, for fear that she will never be able to walk on her own, then I am totally in love with her (the right amount of love) but the quality of that love is smothering or over-connected. In contrast, I might be totally in love with my little boy, but if I cannot bear to hold him in my arms because he resembles my older brother (who was an unkind figure), then I have the right amount of love but, again, the quality is detached, or under-connected.

What about other types of relationships? I may be totally in love with my husband or partner and feel emotionally connected when he is in town but feel insecure when he is out of town on a business trip; then the amount is a good amount of love, but the quality is over-connected or anxious and fearful of loss. Similar to the previous example with the baby, I might feel a lot of good feelings toward my husband or partner, but it just may be that I am not really emotionally connected or can express such positive feelings in only a limited way within this particular relationship. I think you see that in both over- and under-connected relationships, there is an insecurity in the relationship—the insecurity is not about an *individual* being lower in the universal language of love, but the *relationship* being lower in the universal language of love, for it is totally conceivable that the same individual would be and could be different in different relationships.

As examples, consider the following scenarios. Ann may be over-connected with her baby because the baby has a health problem and until that it resolved, she is "on call." Samantha may be under-connected with her baby because she is going through a difficult divorce that leaves her very little energy. Larry might be over-connected with his adult partner because she might find others to love and care for when she goes away to college. Or, Sienna may have some feelings for Carl but not to the extent that she felt for her ex-boyfriend. To put it simply, the universal language of love is about being connected at the moderate level, but nonetheless to feel, as well as to express, the right amount and quality of emotional connection. Being connected in a healthy way is the most important aspect of the universal language of love.

To what types of relationships does the universal language of love refer to? Does it refer to all relationships or only to those in which there is significant value or investment? The answer is, actually, both. The universal language of love can refer to, of course, relationships between those who are related to one another (through birth or adoption) and are in the same family. It can refer to those who have a significant role in the caretaking of our children—for example, child care professionals or foster parents—and our children will love these professionals and these professionals may also love our children.

The universal love language can also be part of other important relationships that have far-reaching value and investment, including, as described earlier, many types of adult-adult relationships, but also where there is an ongoing context of give-and-take. In fact, in a recent presidential election, the nominee (Barack Obama) closed many of his speeches by waving to his supporters, and saying, "I love you" or "I love you back."

Given that the universal language of love is based on scientific research, what does this research show for those who have more of it as opposed to less of it. For this information, we turn mostly to the work on parent-child relationships, the area that has accrued the evidence base in this area. We also highlight areas that deserve attention in this area, as a way to broaden our thinking on this topic.

The research shows that:

- **Children who have emotionally available relationships with their parents are less aggressive and less likely to be the targets of aggression from other children.**

  I recently conducted a study funded by the National Science Foundation on how emotional availability affects children in terms of peer interactions, the child-teacher relationship, and the learning experience. The results state that the emotional connection a parent is able to establish with a child (not just from the parent to the child but from the child back to the parent) before the child is in school is highly predictive of that child's aggression as well as victimization.

  This study involved observing children in classrooms during the kindergarten year. We also asked their teachers to report on child-peer relationships as well as child-teacher relationships. We found that healthy emotional availability between parent and child usually led to less aggression by the child in kindergarten and less victimization of the child by others' aggression. This doesn't mean that the child was never aggressive, nor that other children were never aggressive toward the child; in general, however, the greater the emotional availability in the parent-child relationship, the less likely the child was to be involved in any aggressive episode or dispute with other children. Children from emotionally available relationships used a variety of skills in navigating sources of aggression, including ignoring the children who were aggressive, having clever "comebacks," and the like. It may also be that children in emotionally available relationships with their parents are more emotionally available themselves and therefore have social allies in the classroom who support them during peer interactions.

- **Children from emotionally available homes have better peer relationships.**
  Compared to their peers, such children are more positive and proactively social in interactions with their peers; they are more gracious to others and have a certain air of confidence. These children are more likely to be helpful to other children and seem to sense the feelings of other children and respond in a sensitive manner to them. They are more willing to have positive interactions with their peers, more likely to help out peers, and more likely to respond in a positive or helpful way to any interaction that they begin or respond to with peers. For their futures, children who are emotionally available or whose emotional availability has improved over time will have more skills to understand others and to work with them in collaborative ways. These are important skills for children to learn—as important as their academic learning—because these skills of emotional availability create healthy connections with others in relationships. For children to acquire these skills of emotional availability, they have to be in a network of emotionally available relationships—with their parents, with their teachers, and with others. In such a network, they "feel" what it's like to be in a healthy relationship. They will also likely then contribute to other children's senses of security and emotional availability, thereby enhancing what happens in the community and in society in general.

- **Children who have emotionally available relationships with their parents are more attentive in school.**
  Attentiveness is a very good sign of the capacity for early learning. If a child is attentive and focused on the task at hand, the child is more likely to absorb what is going on in the classroom. However, a child who isn't attentive to the teacher and is easily distracted will not be able to pick up information from the environment.

  In the same National Science Foundation study cited earlier, we observed and scored eye movements of children for a whole year as a measure of attentiveness and lack of distractibility in school. We discovered that children from emotionally available parent-child relationships were more attentive than other children while the teacher was teaching. Emotional availability also appears to be related to teacher-rated academic competence.

  In addition, emotional availability appears to mitigate the effects of some learning problems. Even though learning disabilities are inborn in many ways, learning problems also can be related to the level of emotional connection. Children are less able to concentrate on what is going on in school if they are busy thinking about problems at home. If they are emotionally satisfied and fulfilled at home, however, they come to school ready to learn and are able to concentrate on school instead of being preoccupied with other issues. Interestingly, we find this relation between emotional availability and observed attentiveness in school even when we take into account the effects of a child's age-related language ability. Even younger children with fewer language skills from emotionally available environments exhibit more attentiveness to the teacher. A healthy, emotionally available home life prepares our children to pay attention and concentrate in school.

We also have some evidence that emotional availability is related to knowledge of vocabulary words and of humanities, even after we take into account the child's language level. We theorize that this is because emotionally available parents are more likely to talk to their children and be involved with them at many different levels, emotionally as well as intellectually. The links related to socioeconomic background have not yet been fully studied.

- **Children from emotionally available homes seem to relate better to their teachers.**
  If emotional availability in the parent-child relationship is high, the teacher-child relationship in the school has fewer "bumps," so to speak. That is, children from higher EA families experience less conflict than other children and show less dependence, and the teacher is less likely to see such children as "problems" in the classroom. Basically, teachers are more likely to see those children as allies or kids who are "on the right track." Such children are less likely to be the ones getting the negative attention in the classroom. These findings have major import for our understanding of school readiness. We should be thinking about preparing our children for school many years before they actually set foot into the doors of any formal institution. Our children's preparation begins at the time of birth, and the emotional availability in one's early environment is one of the most important ingredients in that preparation.

- **Infants and children who have emotionally available relationships with their parents are more likely to also show secure bonding or emotional attachment, as measured in other scientifically validated ways.**

Emotionally available interactions during the first year of life and beyond create attachment security in children, with all the positives that such a secure pathway affords.

- **Twenty to thirty percent of mother-child relationships in normal, unselected families are in the gray to dark zone of emotional availability.**
This percentage is about 50 percent in child-child care professional relationships. The percentage of emotional availability in our relationships is an intriguing area to explore in different societies. Some societies may view emotional availability as crucial, whereas others may view it as less important in their lives. This is not about abuse, neglect, or even obvious rejection, but about the expressions of the universal language of love.

Most parents are generally involved and caring—the problem arises when the parents' version of "good enough" parenting and the children's point of view of the same thing are different. If children aren't feeling emotionally connected to their parents, the consequences can be subtle yet pervasive. Emotionally unavailable parenting predisposes children to unhappiness or being emotionally shut down and may create either emotional disconnection or unhealthy emotional over-connection with the very people who care most about them—their parents. We can potentially make similar statements about child care professionals and the children they care for. For example, a problem can arise if the child care professional's version of "good enough" caregiving and the children's point of view of the same thing are different. Emotionally available caregiving in child care can maintain a solid sense of emotional security or even improve a child's sense of security if such security and trust are not present in the family, but an emotionally distant climate in a child care site can make children suffer, either silently or outwardly.

In the area of adult-adult relationships, similar thinking is there.[1] If both individuals in an ongoing relationship or interaction can be really emotionally available to each other, then the relationship is more rewarding for both. If one of them is unavailable emotionally, however, then it is important to recognize or be aware of this expression in the universal language of love.

---

[1]Statistics for relationships other than that of child-caretaker are not available.

If you would like to read the scientific research on emotional availability, please visit www.emotionalavailability.com for a list of selected publications. You will find research on depression, substance abuse, developmental disabilities, attachment, cognitive competence, and numerous other topics in relation to emotional availability. As well, for more information on our training on the EA assessments and/or interventions (parents or professionals), please visit this website.

# 2 Understanding the Six Dimensions of the Universal Language of Love in Caregiver-Child Relationships

This chapter will help you to understand the six dimensions of the universal language of love in caregiver-child relationships. Typically, we assess emotional availability/unavailability in a clinical or research laboratory setting. If the dyad is a baby and parent, we provide some age-appropriate toys and leave them to play on the floor, saying, "Play as you normally do." We film about a half hour in the laboratory. Particularly with babies, we often go into the home with a camcorder, and say, "Go about your normal daily routine." We have filmed parents and children in various scenarios: as the parent is vacuuming, during a feeding, during bath time, as well as during play. We like to get a variety of contexts so that we have a sense of what the normal day is like for them. Because the contexts in the home can be so varied, our observations sometimes last an hour or two. For preschoolers we usually see families in the laboratory. Typically, we have the child and parent play together, such as for about 5 minutes with Etch-A-Sketch, with the parent operating the vertical dial and the child operating the horizontal dial. The task is to cooperatively draw a boat or a house. A model sketch is usually presented to them. They then are asked to engage in fantasy play with some toys that include knights and princesses and other parts to evoke imaginative play (usually 20 minutes). Similar contexts are used with older children. The idea is always to provide some age-appropriate toys and to videotape the dyad as they play.

At all ages, including babies, we also like to film, if at all possible, the parent and child in a stressful context. An example would be after a "reunion," in which the parent has been out of the room for a few minutes, leaving the child with an adult stranger, and then comes back into the room. Such a reunion can give us much interesting information about how the

9

baby or young child reacts to the parent under stress—this is sometimes very telling about whether the baby or child feels comfortable going to the parent for support during a time of stress. Although separation-reunion is the most commonly used context to understand adult-child relationships under stress, other stressful contexts are and should be noteworthy.

Child care is an enormously important time for babies and children. Because of the extensive time that many children spend with child care professionals, and the emotional bonds that can and should form, child care professionals are likely attachment figures in a child's life. Thus, most of the same principles of the language of love apply here as well. Therefore, at times we are interested in the relationship between a nonparental caregiver and a child, as for example, a child care professional and a child. We have found in our scientific work that these relationships can differ, partly because there are numerous children, and often numerous adults, in the same setting. So, just as having more than one child in the home changes the nature of the relationship between a parent and a child, the child care context is also what we call more "distributed" as a form of emotional connection.

Even though the relationship between a specific child care professional and a specific child might be affected by the number and types of children and the number and types of child care staff, nonetheless specific emotional relationships are being formed and being maintained. It therefore makes sense for us to think about the universal language of love when we talk about child care.

Our research evaluates adult-child relationships (parent-child, child care professional-child, or other adult-child) by separating its qualities into six dimensions. We score each quality on a numbered scale. These principles are what clinicians, researchers, and other child psychologists look for when they are evaluating an adult-child relationship directly. To conduct this assessment, we observe the adult-child relationship. To conduct your own assessment, you can observe your own relationship with your child, or that of someone close to you, such as your partner. You can also observe the relationship of your friends or relatives with their children, all with this powerful and robust tool, backed by 20 years of science in more than 20 different countries.

Some of these principles measure the presence of a particular trait or attitude (sensitivity, structuring), a couple of them measure the absence of such traits (nonhostility and nonintrusiveness), and still others evaluate the child's behavior with the adult.

All relationships are two-way streets; often the most telling evaluation of the quality of the connection lies not with the adult's immediate actions but with the child's response. How the child reacts to the adult makes the difference between a high- and low-quality emotional connection between the two. The reason for this is that the child carries the "history" of the relationship with him or her.

This history of relationships is most telling in the case of parent-child relationships in which the two share a consistent and full history. Often, however, children have been adopted or are in foster care, and the family and the child do not share at least a part of their history. How do we evaluate and think about the language of love then? And what about the scenarios of children who spend a significant portion of their time in child care with at least one other adult? Or what about the scenarios of children who are separated from a parent (due to divorce or due to military deployments) while they are in a relationship with another adult? Finally, what about when a child has lost a parent by death and may show this sense of loss in the relationship with the remaining parent? How do we observe and understand these complex relationships that are becoming increasingly more common in today's society?

What we and others find in the scientific work on the universal language of love is that regardless of the reason, we can look at where we really are in a relationship *today*. Where we are today is not necessarily all due to us because, as noted, the history may not be all ours. Even as a parent, part of the way a baby interacts and reacts is based on this baby's history, which may and may not include you, but includes all of the people this baby has known in some way. For a child who has been exposed to drugs, alcohol, or nicotine in utero and adopted into a loving home, the relationship includes the new family as well as the prior biochemical history in the womb. Similarly, a child coming into child care brings with him or her the history of home life. If it has been a secure and fun-filled home, the child is likely to expect this in the child care setting and, in fact, evoke it in the new caregivers. If, on the other hand, a child comes from a violent and unpredictable household, he or she may come to expect disorganization and chaos in other relationships. This expectation may be fulfilled, as child care professionals are at their wits' end to react to and cope with an aggressive child who has difficulty with self-regulation. Still, in a similar vein, when a family is breaking up, any child will feel pain, and this pain can be expressed in the relationships with parents, teachers, friends, or others.

The universal language of love is about realistically looking at the current relationship and then moving from there to enhance it. It is not about blaming and it is not even about assessing a pure relationship between one individual and another. Relationships affect other relationships, and relationships occur in the context of other relationships. Nonetheless, we have been able to look at relationships one at a time, from the adult's side and then from the child's side, and then we put it together to understand the language of love that is being voiced.

> I say "voiced" rather than "spoken" because babies cannot speak but they also have a voice, and this voice is clear in their actions and in their babbles and in their cries. They clearly are a part of the language of love in all families and in all settings!

I have posed the six principles of emotional availability for the child-caretaker relationship in the form of questions. I have deliberately used the same questions that form the basis of emotional availability research in clinical settings, simply because the terms are recognized and accepted throughout the field of psychology. Later, these six principles will be explored for adult-adult relationships. By asking yourself these questions, corresponding to the six principles of emotional availability, you can assess the quality of your own emotional connection with each of the children in your life, be it in your personal life or in a professional capacity. These six questions are:

1. How sensitive are you in this relationship?
2. Do you structure interactions appropriately?
3. Are you available in this relationship without being intrusive?
4. Is there any overt or covert hostility present?
5. Is this child responsive to you?
6. Does this child allow you to be involved in his or her life?

# 1. How Sensitive Are You in This Relationship?

Sensitivity is the adult's ability to "read" a child and be emotionally and openly communicative with that child. Sensitivity is the tool that allows an individual to create a strong emotional connection. It refers to a variety of qualities in the adult, such as responsiveness, accurate reading of a child's communications, ability to resolve conflicts smoothly, and so on. When an individual is sensitive to a child's needs, this individual can come up with the response that is appropriate to the moment. This usually makes the child feel loved, supported, and connected because the child's cues and communications have been read.

> Sarah's 1-year-old daughter, Meg, is just beginning to walk. We observed their interactions for about an hour in our clinic. It was obvious that Sarah was sensitive to her daughter's emotional and physical needs. When Meg would bring Sarah a block or play toy, Sarah would respond warmly, admiring the toy and asking Meg questions about it. Both the tone of Sarah's voice and her clear interest in Meg's activities were sincere and appropriate (i.e., not overenthusiastic or false). When Meg toddled away to investigate something on her own, Sarah chatted casually with the researcher while still keeping an eye on her daughter. After a while, Meg started getting frustrated with the wooden train she was playing with—she couldn't get it to move. Noticing Meg's frustration, Sarah went over and checked in with her daughter, asking, "What is it, honey?" She then offered her another toy. After playing with Sarah for a few minutes, the child went off exploring again, and Sarah returned to her seat.

Sarah's responses showed she knew her daughter well and was attuned to her physical and emotional needs. She was comfortable letting Meg explore on her own, but she also was interested and connected with whatever her daughter was doing. She didn't overwhelm Meg with false attention or emotion; she also was able to diffuse the potential frustration about the toy quickly, and move the child on to other activities. Sarah is an excellent example of a sensitive adult.

Infants and young children often cannot tell us what they want and need in words, but they do communicate nonverbally. This includes communication about their emotional needs as well as their physical ones. When Meg came to Sarah to show her the toy, it was obvious that she wanted her mother's attention. However, Sarah also picked up the subtler signal of Meg's frustration with the train and the need for some help and/or redirection.

> Many parents are very good at deciphering their children's nonverbal cues, whether it be facial expression, body language, behavioral cues, or others.

According to one mother, when her son comes home from school, she can tell in a minute whether it's been a good or bad day. When he's had a bad day, he gets this furrow between his eyebrows. Even when he tries to tell her everything's okay, if that furrow is there she knows something's up. She doesn't push him about it, but after they chat for a while, he'll usually clue her in to what's going on.

Some of the most important nonverbal clues are signals of avoidance because they are signs that the child is becoming emotionally unrecruitable. Moms report, "My baby doesn't come to me enough," "I wish my baby were more affectionate to me," or "My baby would rather play by himself than with me." But they don't interpret these behaviors as signs that their children are feeling a lack of connection with them. Many parents take the view, "Well, my baby's just like that; it's his [or her] temperament [or genetics]." But in our research, we see children of all temperaments being responsive or unresponsive. Often, when there's a problem with a parent's level of emotional recruitability, we see the child being more responsive with one parent than the other.

Of course, no parent or caregiver can be attuned to a child at all times; everyone misses signals every now and then. It's the overall level of sensitivity to a child that is important. When we measure sensitivity in a clinical setting, we look at a variety and number of parent-child interactions over a period of time rather than examining one particular instance. You should do the same when assessing your own sensitivity. Here are some of the key traits of an adult who is sensitive to his or her child:

- *Predominantly positive, in terms of both facial and vocal expressiveness.* Especially when dealing with infants and preverbal children, an adult's facial expression and voice are what communicate the level of emotional connection. A sensitive adult is predominantly positive rather than bored, discontented, or harsh.

> Paul works at home, and it is his job to pick up his son, Ethan, from preschool each day at noon, get him lunch, and then put him down for his nap. Although Paul's work as a graphic designer can be very demanding, he makes this time with Ethan their special time. He is attuned to his son's moods and needs, and is good at responding to both verbal and nonverbal cues. In contrast, Paul's wife, Deborah, who is an attorney, is not

particularly sensitive to Ethan. She admits that too often she "brings her day home" with her, and her fatigue causes her to respond harshly to Ethan's demands for her attention. Even when she means to be warm and caring, her face doesn't communicate her emotions well. Sensing this, Ethan turns more to his father than his mother for emotional support and connection.

- *Appropriately responsive to the circumstances and the child's emotions.*
  If you laugh and smile at everything this child does, you will come across as unauthentic and not spontaneous. Indeed, it is often inappropriate to be positive to everything, as this would seem more like a performance than real emotion. A general positive attitude is more important as long as it is genuine and emotionally based.

  > Carl, a divorced father with two children from a previous marriage, vowed that he would be a better father when he and his second wife had their daughter, Lisa. But if you ask most observers, they'll tell you that Carl tries too hard. Lisa, who's seven, is involved in gymnastics, and whenever Carl sees her do anything—a somersault, a back bend, a cartwheel—he praises her enthusiastically and extravagantly. But his response is inappropriate for the level of achievement, and Lisa knows it. It feels false to everyone but Carl, who thinks he's being a "good parent."

  If Carl were more sensitive to Lisa's needs, he could offer support and encouragement in a more genuine way, at a level of positive emotion appropriate to what Lisa is experiencing. This would create a stronger sense of connection between father and daughter.

- *Displaying congruence between verbal and nonverbal expression.*
  If an adult's words are caring, but there is no warmth in the face or voice, what part of the message do you think a child receives more clearly?

  > Joanna has three children under the age of five. She tries to be warm and caring with her children, but she is frequently preoccupied with household tasks. When her 5-year-old son, Brandon, proudly shows her his latest drawing, she responds, "That's beautiful, dear! Why don't you put it on the

refrigerator?" However, she barely looks at the paper and her voice sounds distracted.

Brandon is confused: he's getting one message from his mother's words and another from her tone and actions. Joanna is trying to be sensitive to her child but can't. This kind of pseudosensitivity creates confusion for the child.

Jim is a big, bluff, hearty kind of guy who came from a family that always teased each other unmercifully. When he had a son, Jim's idea of affection was to croon to his son, "Jimmy, you're a little stinker, you know that? How'd you get to be soooo ugly?" Jim's adult friends found this to be funny, but as his son Jimmy grew older and started to understand the words his dad was using to express his affection, he grew confused and started to turn away from Jim. Jim, on his part, didn't understand what was going on. "I'm just teasing the kid!" he'd protest. "Can't he take a joke?"

Yes, he could—if Jimmy were old enough to understand that his father's tone and emotion were genuine and the words were meant to be funny. The sensitive parent expresses the emotion he or she wants to communicate through words, facial expressions, and vocal tones. The child should get one message, rather than being confused by conflicts between verbal and nonverbal communication.

- *Accurately perceptive and appropriately responsive.*
Being sensitive means you can read this child's signals and communication accurately, and then respond in a manner appropriate to this child and the situation.

Emily was nanny to a two-year-old deaf girl named Sydney in her home. It was delightful to watch them together: Emily was clearly attuned to Sydney's needs, discerning when the little girl became bored with the puzzle she was working with and moving her smoothly on to another activity. Emily could "read" Sydney's emotional cues with ease and accuracy, and respond appropriately to this child's needs.

Karen became a mother when she was 16 years old, and her own immaturity seemed to prevent her from interacting appropriately with her son, Matthew, age 4. When another little boy started a fight with Matthew on the playground, Karen came up to Matthew and jerked him away. "You're always getting into trouble!" she scolded him. She didn't notice that Matthew wasn't responsible for starting the fight. Matthew protested and then started to cry, which caused Karen to snap, "Stop that. You're a big boy now, and big boys don't cry."

Because Karen rushed to a conclusion, her perception was not accurate.

- *Aware of timing.*
During the course of a day, or simply an afternoon, adults and children interact in many ways—playing, feeding, bathing, joint "chores," and so on. When it comes to assessing sensitivity to a child, the timing of many of these activities may be more important than the content. Children rely on a sense of rhythm and progression in their days—they need some kind of order to provide a sense of security and safety. Sensitive adults are careful not to introduce abrupt transitions between activities. For example, they soothe the baby before they put him or her down for a nap.

Awareness of timing becomes even more critical with older children and teenagers. Knowing when to broach difficult subjects or ask questions is a vital parenting skill.

Chuck knew that his teenage daughter, Mary, had an important math test coming up. Math wasn't Mary's strong suit, and Chuck wanted to help her, but he also knew that Mary hated to admit she needed help in any subject. The week before the test, Mary brought an English paper home and proudly showed it to her father. She had received an A+. Chuck praised her highly, read a little of the paper, and commented on how well she had expressed herself. Then he said, "I always did really well in math and science when I was in high school, but I could never write compositions. I was really grateful that my mom was so good at writing. She checked stuff over for me and helped me out with my English papers. And I always looked over the checkbook for her to make sure her math was right!" After they both laughed, Mary admitted she wasn't as good at math as she was at English, and mentioned the upcoming math test. "Maybe I could help you study," Chuck said. "I think I can remember my algebra. I'd sure like to give you a hand if I can."

Because Chuck was sensitive to Mary's emotions, he was able to offer help in a way she could receive it. He also acknowledged her excellence in one area before bringing up discreetly the place where she needed assistance. The timing and manner of his offer showed his emotional sensitivity to his daughter.

- *Flexible in terms of attention, behavior, and approach*
  An adult whose attention is flexible can do other things and still be able to respond appropriately to a child. If the adult's attention is less flexible, the adult "tunes out" when absorbed in a task and "tunes in" only when he or she is ready.

> Instead of requiring Charlie to tell her whenever he needed to urinate or defecate and then standing over him until he did, Alison, the child care professional, told Charlie, "I think you're a big enough boy now that you can start to use the toilet instead of going in a diaper. Let's try this. Whenever you need to go, you tell me, and then you decide whether you want to use the toilet or your diaper. If you want to use the diaper, fine, but if you're ready to go like a big boy, I'll take you to the toilet." Alison also set up a chart on the wall, and every time Charlie used the toilet he got to put a sticker on the chart. Alison had to be very flexible. For the first few weeks Charlie elected to use the diaper a lot more than the toilet. Even when he said he wanted to use the toilet, he sometimes wouldn't make it in time. Alison continued to make toilet training a game, rewarding Charlie when he acted like a "big boy" but encouraging him in whatever choice he made. Even though Charlie took longer to train than some of the other babies, Alison was flexible.
>
> Pat and Arthur have very different styles when it comes to playing games with their kids. In some ways, Pat is just another "big kid." When she plays with her 5-year-old son, she becomes a fireman, a horse, a space man—whatever the game requires. She's very creative, too, suggesting ideas for new story lines and ways to play, but never insisting that her ideas are better than her son's. In contrast, Arthur is far more structured in his interactions with both his 9-year-old daughter and his young son. He insists they follow the rules exactly when

playing board games, and he is clearly uncomfortable when it comes to "pretending." He loves his kids, but he relates to them as he thinks an adult should, rather than being flexible enough to enter into their play in ways that connect on the level of just having fun, and seems less emotionally available than Pat, or even emotionally unavailable.

Linked to flexibility in play is another trait of the sensitive adult: variety and creativity in modes of play. How willing you are to join in a child's activities in a playful rather than didactic (teaching) way can be a profound language of love, even for teachers and child care professionals who may be very invested in teaching.

- *Showing acceptance of the child.*
A more sensitive adult typically speaks to a child as if he or she were a separate, respectable person with clear needs, wishes, and goals. Even with very young children, a sensitive adult will offer choices, ask the child's opinion, and be willing to accommodate the child's requests within reason. A sensitive adult also holds conversations with the child, even a baby. A baby understands a great deal of nonverbal communication and grows with verbal conversations. A sensitive adult will generally describe actions to the baby, helping the infant to be a part of the adult's view of the world. Conversely, a more insensitive adult may make disparaging or unaccepting comments either to or about the child, sometimes in the form of jokes or offhand remarks.

Ever since Katherine's daughter, Anne, turned 12, there has been a lot of friction between them. Anne wants to dress like Britney Spears, while her mother wants to keep her in little-girl jumpers and ankle socks. Katherine insists that Anne is still a child, makes fun of Anne's attempts to mimic the artists on MTV, refuses to allow her to try on lipstick at home, and refers to the afternoons Anne spends with her best friend, Cynthia, as "playdates."

Katherine is having a difficult time accepting that her daughter is growing up, and she refuses to offer the emotional support Anne could use, even if she does not approve of some of her choices. If Katherine simply recognized that Anne is changing from a child to a young woman and acknowledged her awareness of the differences, Anne would be less likely to want to "grow up" even faster than she is. With a little awareness and emotional support on Katherine's part, this could be a time when mother and daughter become closer, a closeness that would serve both of them well as Anne enters her teen years.

- *Empathic*—*"putting one's self in the child's shoes."*
Empathy is the ability to take the perspective of the other and to feel what he or she feels. Much of sensitivity is about empathic understanding of the child. With a toddler, the sensitive adult is empathic of a child's issues with autonomy and/or with tantrums. With an older child, the sensitive caregiver is empathic about problems with peers. The sensitive parent is able to feel empathy for the plight of the child and about the trials and tribulations of growing up. Thus, the empathic adult refrains from shaming, or belittling, and instead helps a child to understand his or her feelings.

> A well-known writer noted in her diary that when her young son was barely 6, she had left him with her ex-husband, the boy's father, for an extended period while she pursued additional studies in a foreign country. She felt this was a wonderful arrangement because her son's basic needs would surely be taken care of, and she would have her freedom to pursue her goals without interruption. She wrote in the diary that she rarely thought about her son, but did have a dream one night that she was speaking with her child and how he was listening to her problems and her emotional issues and was so utterly empathic aobut his mother's life and her needs. It appears this writer came first and wanted caregiving for herself, rather than being empathic about her son's own emotional needs.

- *Able to handle conflict.*
How conflict situations are handled is a very clear indicator of the degree of adult sensitivity. No caregiver is perfect, and a certain amount of conflict or mismatched interactions between a caregiver and child is normal. It is common to see adult insistence on a goal (helping to clear the table, for example) meet child resistance (Melissa wants to watch TV instead). How adults and children move from conflict to more harmonious states is as important as the quality of the harmonious state itself. With a sensitive adult and child, conflicts are usually resolved with negotiation and co-determination of outcomes (Melissa will help clear the table for five minutes before her show comes on). If the adult is

less sensitive, insistence and resistance provoke rising levels of anger and frustration. The adult finds it difficult to relinquish control and/or to give credence to the goals and desires of the child. The result is something like: "Clear the table right now, young lady, or you won't see any TV tonight!" from the adult, and then the child feels frustrated and powerless and may break a few dishes "by accident."

Sensitive adults don't have to demonstrate their emotions in a certain way. They may be soft-spoken or animated, gentle or strong, low-keyed or vivacious. Often men and women have completely different styles when it comes to being sensitive to their children. The real test is not so much the style of the adults, but their willingness to be attuned to the needs, desires, and goals of children, and to express themselves in an emotionally connected manner.

> **The ability to hear the voices of the children you are with and give them the feeling that you understand them is what it's all about.**

- Many adults, including teachers, know that it can be difficult to "read" an adolescent but that they need to try anyway. Babies have voices that need to be heard also. Listen to and understand the emotional signals and communications of a relationship with a baby as well as a child or teen. Long before there is clear verbal give and take, your child or a child you are working with is telling you what he or she needs. We merely need to listen and understand.

- An adult cannot be sensitive without the child. Sensitivity is looking to the child's experience of you and adjusting your behavior accordingly. When you are able to see and hear the child, not just "hear" yourself in the interaction, then you are truly sensitive in this relationship.

- Is this a fun relationship for the two of you? Nothing is a better indicator of the health of any caregiver-child relationship!

## 2. Do You Structure Interactions Appropriately?

In our research studies, we found that caregivers who structure well (e.g., breaking up play tasks into smaller pieces, setting limits) may actually seem to be providing few clues and suggestions to the child, but the child almost automatically picks up such suggestions. It indicates that a caregiver has an intimate knowledge of what works in this relationship. In the context of multiple children, and potentially multiple caregivers, structuring becomes an even more important quality to master, a part of our tool kit for expressing the language of love. In fact, our scientific work has shown that in the child care context, structuring is really all-important, perhaps because this is a key way to express the language of love when there are so many things going on.

> The more going on for a family or in the context, the more important the role of structuring as part of our EA tool kit.

## Structuring during Play

Structuring is not about guiding every moment; rather, it is about providing a supportive frame in a relaxed, unforced way. In a child care setting, it may mean providing activities in one area that a number of children can join. In the home, it may be making suggestions about the ongoing play activities.

Optimal structuring usually has both verbal and nonverbal components. Using more than one form of communication helps to give a child a greater range of clues and tips about engaging the play materials. Conversely, adults who are following the lead of their children and letting the children structure a particular game or other play must attune themselves to the verbal and nonverbal clues the children are providing. Sometimes a child will tell his preschool teacher, "Mrs. Sandy, you're not playing the game right!" but more often there will be nonverbal hints of the child's wanting to take the game in a different direction.

During playtime with a child, the adult who understands how to structure offers guidance but not direction. The adult is an active participant in the play, providing information, breaking down steps to help the child complete a puzzle or game or task, and physically helping the child when the child wants it (but not until then). Such individuals may allow the child to win the game or diminish the importance of adult victory.

> Connie was delighted when Alexander, her 6-year-old son, declared, "I want to learn how to play chess!" Connie had played the game all her life, and had entered a few tournaments in high school. She wanted to make sure, however, that Alexander regarded chess as a game, not as a competition between them.

Connie explained to Alexander what the different chess pieces were, and then showed him how to set up the board. Then she took him through a few basic moves, explaining how each piece moves in a different way. She made the game into a story about gallant knights, valiant pawns, sneaky bishops, gracious queens, and powerful kings. She let Alexander make his own moves, seldom offering advice but making sure he remembered the basics of the game. At age 6, Alexander's attention span was limited, so they played together only as long as he remained interested in the game. The more he understood, the more interested he became. Connie deliberately let Alexander win the first few games they completed. After that, she would occasionally win a game and explain how she did so.

Connie's goal was to foster her son's interest in chess and to share her love of the game with him. Because she was able to structure his experience of chess in ways appropriate to his age, attention span, and abilities, Alexander grew to love and appreciate the game. The relationship between mother and son was also deepened by their common interest, but more important, by their emotional connection during the process of learning.

From the time she could walk, Sonny always loved messing around the kitchen while her live-in grandma, Louise, cooked. As the child grew older, she demanded that Louise let her "help" with the cooking. Louise was very careful to give Sonny specific tasks appropriate to her age. She had her put rice into a cup and then use a spatula to level off the top. She asked Sonny to mash up a cooked egg yolk with a fork, and then put the paste into the potato salad Louise was making. As Sonny grew older, she learned how to beat eggs, measure flour, roll out cookie dough, and so on. Louise always gave Sonny specific instructions, showed her how to carry them out when necessary, and then thanked her for her help. Eventually Louise could tell Sonny, "I need three eggs beaten, and then mixed into the ground beef for the meat loaf," and be confident that Sonny could handle it. Louise also gave food safety-related structuring, such as telling Sonny not to put the raw egg or meat into her mouth and to make sure she washed her hands thoroughly.

By the time Sonny was 7, she was making simple cakes

and side dishes on her own, with her grandmother offering the occasional suggestion. Louise created a favorable structure in which Sonny could learn more and more about an activity she enjoyed—cooking—at levels appropriate for her age and abilities. The structure also helped Louise enjoy the experience of teaching a little girl, thus strengthening the connection between the two. Interestingly, and not surprisingly, Sonny and her mother, Albertha, continued these activities when Albertha came home from work. Although Louise grew up in a different generation, she learned the universal language of love and helped her grandchild to grow and feel a secure and consistent emotional connection within the family.

One of the most important components of structuring is providing a supportive frame in which the child has a chance to explore and try new things. We as adults have to allow children room and space to grow, and any structure we establish must be flexible enough to give children increasing amounts of autonomy. Good structuring is like a scaffold: Within it, children can climb higher and higher, learning more and more, confident that there is a solid framework to support them every step along the way.

## *Structuring by Limit Setting*

Individuals who feel they always need to be liked may have a difficult time with setting limits. They don't want to risk alienating the child by setting limits. A great way to set limits is to first have an emotional connection with a child, and that emotional connection can really be forged through play. The more you play and interact with a child or your group of children, the more you can expect that each child will listen to your limits. Because you have joined the child's world, the child (or group) will return the favor.

Research has shown that children who are raised in an emotionally connected yet consistently structured environment have less drug use, less promiscuity, and get better grades. Further, the more adults in a child's life who speak the language of love, the more likely that the child will reap the rewards from such an emotionally available community! An important aspect of the language of love, shown universally to be related to positive outcomes for children, is structuring, in the form of limit setting and discipline! It is important for all adults to provide appropriate rules and regulations (depending on a child's age and stage of development) and then stick by them. Limit setting is about rules and regulations—it's about law and order. But, to help a child succeed, the adults in a child's life need to let the child know what those are, but also to be preventive. Remember that toddlers like to explore, and so rather than having to tell a toddler, "Don't touch" all the pretty knickknacks in Grandma's house, you might very quietly remove everything breakable that might be within reach during a visit.

In the case of structuring and limit-setting behaviors, too much or too little are equally bad. Even inconsistent structuring can be difficult for a child. Individuals who create a certain framework of structure but then back off at the first challenge or difficulty leave children feeling as though they can't trust the structure—the scaffold isn't steady beneath their feet. Some adults over-structure in some circumstances (around school or drugs or sex, for example) and completely lack structure in other circumstances (not asking the child to do homework, or unconcerned about when the child gets home for dinner). In these cases, discipline and limit setting are inconsistent, with predictable results. Children who are faced with inconsistent structure are getting mixed messages, and often they respond with confusion, frustration, and potentially defiance. They also may learn to value certain things, such as staying away from drugs, but not value other things, such as doing homework diligently.

> Not too long ago, a teenage girl, Brittany, was referred to me as a real discipline problem. She had a history of problems in school, was abusing alcohol, and had become pregnant. The mother, Beth, accompanied her daughter to the session and complained, "I don't know why she's so wild. I never asked anything of any of my kids. The only thing I ever demanded of them was that they go to church on Sunday and not take the Lord's name in vain." She also described a household in which there were no rules or expectations for positive behavior.

Beth had a lot of rules and structure around religion, but provided almost no structure in any other part of her children's lives. Brittany interpreted this as meaning that her mother didn't really care about her. It's no wonder Brittany acted out and ran wild.

Kids need structure and limits. They need boundaries, if only to have something to push against so they know they're growing. But structure can be perceived as either jail bars or scaffolding, depending on how it's done by parents. While structuring may not be the most pleasant part of emotional availability, when parents can set frameworks for their children in a supportive and caring way, children will feel secure, focused, and happy.

> Eight-year-old Todd was a child who always pushed the boundaries set for him. He rode his bike farther and faster than anyone; he climbed higher trees than any of his friends. But his parents were always firm when it came to the rules around Todd's behavior. He wasn't to endanger himself or others, he wasn't to stay out late without calling first, and he was to act in a responsible manner when it came to his 5-year-old brother, Mike.
>
> One day Todd got caught up in a game he was playing with his friends, and he left the playground, not telling Mike where he was going. Mike, who was busy on the monkey bars, didn't notice Todd was gone until 20 minutes later. He looked around for his older brother for about 10 minutes, and then started to cry. A neighbor noticed Mike's distress and drove the boy home.
>
> When Todd came home later, his dad asked him what had happened. Todd admitted he had forgotten about Mike. "My friends and I wanted to ride bikes and so we left," he said.
>
> "Todd, I know you want to be with your friends, and most of the time that's just fine. But Mike's not old enough to ride bikes, and you were supposed to be keeping an eye on him," his dad replied. "Mike was really scared when he realized you weren't there. You know that leaving Mike alone broke a rule. So no bike riding for a week, and when you're done at school this week, you're to come straight home every day."
>
> "No fair!" Todd protested.
>
> "Sorry, Todd, but it is fair. In the future, if you aren't able to keep an eye on Mike, you can bring him home before you go off with your friends."

Todd's dad did a great job of providing structure. The rules for Todd were clear, simple, and easy to follow. They allowed Todd room to be active and explore while still demanding that he be responsible. When the rules were broken, the consequences were also clear, immediate, and appropriate to the violation. The punishment was meted out without a lot of emotion or hostility on the father's part. This kind of structuring allowed both Todd and his father to feel comfortable and confident in their relationship with each other.

> ## Structuring is just as important as "being nice" or "being kind."

Many individuals do not realize that structuring is a crucial ingredient of the universal language of love. To express love, individuals also need to appropriately control and set boundaries, which is what structuring is!

- Many adults realize that to be sensitive, you need to read your child's signals and communications, but they are surprised that to structure during play, they again need the same skill and inclination. As we play with children, not only do we need to make sure we are following their lead rather than the other way around, but we also need to provide well-appointed suggestions and participate in their play.

- Playing is an important beginning because you need to know a child to know how to structure him or her. Without enough one-on-one play, being close is not as feasible. That half hour a day would be the most desired slot of time. If you are a child care professional, still "schedule" some playtime with each of the children in your care; for example, some time with Tommy at drop-off first thing in the morning when there aren't that many children in yet, and another with Tommy right before nap, and so on. This way, you get to have some magical time with each of the children in your care.

- During play, and at other times, the adult should be a participant rather than a removed and distant presence. How do you become a participant? One of the nicest techniques you can use is to "describe" rather than prohibit. If you see a child do something he or she should not be doing, rather than saying, "Don't" or "I told you not to do that," or other such intrusions, merely describe. For example, if he or she is about to put a wet glass near the TV monitor, say, "Sweetie, you are about to put a wet glass near the TV." If he or she is killing one dinosaur with another during play, say, "The dinosaurs are fighting." These comments are descriptive, and make your child feel that you are a participant without being judgmental or prohibitive. They make you emotionally present, yet nonintrusive.

- Structure play that is appropriate to your child's age and development. Teaching over a child's head or setting overly strict or overly lax and permissive limits is less likely to help than setting clear, understandable, and consistent limits. Structure play by giving a "gentle push" appropriate to the child's age, but do not "take over."

- Our studies have indicated that structuring becomes particularly important as children approach school age. Children who have been structured well during play do better in school in a variety of ways. So, along with sensitivity, structuring provides a child with a sense of trust and support.

- Just as with sensitivity, nonhostility, and the other components of emotional availability, it is important to be consistent. It builds trust!

- Limit setting is often difficult for adults, particularly those who have a deep need to be liked. What adults don't realize sometimes is that children can find other peers—they need adults to set limits. Children like limits because they instinctively know that adults struggle with setting limits. Such struggle is appreciated and is a sign of caring—because it takes work!

- Our studies also show interesting links between the different components of emotional availability. For example, adults who structure their children's interactions and set appropriate limits also seem to manage their own aggressive impulses well (i.e., they are nonhostile and peaceful adults). It is likely that such adults instinctively know or have learned that they need to contain child misbehaviors, and if the children are the ones who have the control, adults respond by being hostile. It is easier to be peaceful with a child who listens to you than a child who is defiant. A subtle nod is often acknowledged by some children. To get the effect and expectations you want, play! The more you join a child's world, the more you can expect in terms of attentiveness to your requests.

## 3. Are You Available in This Relationship without Being Intrusive?

Intrusive behavior can take many forms. If adults set the pace and tone of interactions too often, this can be intrusive. Asking too many questions, directing the course of play rather than letting the child take the lead, making suggestions, and creating frequent theme changes are all indicative of intrusion into a child's autonomy.

One of the ways in which we see adult intrusiveness is with over-stimulation. For example, during physical play with a child, the adult might get rougher and rougher until the child reacts adversely. Over-stimulation is a frequent risk with babies, especially for first-time parents. It's all too easy for well-meaning new parents to play with the baby too much, make too many cute faces when the baby is looking away (a signal the child has had enough), pick the baby up and jiggle him or her when the baby is tired, change the position of the baby for no particular reason, and so on. It takes practice to learn to read a child's cues, and to recognize when the baby or child wants to interact with you and when it's time to leave him or her alone.

As the child goes from infant to toddler stage, intrusiveness can take the opposite direction. Instead of over-stimulating, the parent becomes overprotective. For example, a parent who doesn't allow a normal, well-developing preschooler the chance to walk up and down stairs might be considered intrusive. However, the determination of intrusiveness depends upon the child's level of development. A 1-year-old child may not be ready for the stairs, but a 2-year-old may be. Cutting up your 5-year-old's food is definitely intrusive, but at 1 or even 2, you'd better take charge of the knife if you want to avert the possibility of disaster.

The other way that intrusiveness can manifest is in overdirectiveness. Children have to be given room in which to experiment for themselves; an overly directive adult does not allow the child to develop his or her potential. Some adults spend a lot of time directing their children to accomplish certain activities, "helping" them to succeed at games, and "showing" them the best ways to do things. In extreme cases, overdirectiveness can take the form of physically moving, pushing, or manhandling the child.

> Sally wanted to teach her granddaughter, Kim, to knit. She had tried several times, but the little girl couldn't seem to get the hang of it. Sally talked her through each step, her voice getting louder and louder as her frustration increased. Finally, Sally took Kim's hands in her own and "showed" her how to make stitches correctly. Kim burst into tears and said, "I don't want to learn to knit!" Instead of a chance to develop a deeper emotional connection with her grandchild, Sally's intrusiveness had made the knitting lesson a source of upset for both her and Kim.

The reasons behind adult intrusiveness can be conscious or unconscious, and include traits such as:

- *An overdeveloped need to control the environment.*
  This can be a reflection of obsessive-compulsive tendencies on the part of the adult. If the child does not do things exactly as the adult would like them done (as in the example of Sally and Kim), criticism or perpetual corrections may be the result.

- *Viewing the role of adult as that of a teacher.*
  This can often arise with adults, who feel the children they take care of have to "catch up" developmentally, emotionally, or educationally, or a combination of all three. We sometimes see such behavior in foster parents who feel that their role is to teach and help a child catch up.

  > Dan, an artist, uses every opportunity to teach his foster son, Kevin, about art, instructing him on the proper use of line, color, shape, form, and texture. Unfortunately, Kevin isn't interested in technique—he just likes using paints and crayons. Dan's efforts to teach his foster son continually backfires as Kevin gets bored and Dan gets frustrated. Dan's overdirectiveness creates a great deal of tension between father and foster son.

- *Subtle or not-so-subtle personality dysfunctions.*
  An adult with narcissistic tendencies (read "self-centered") might want a child to stop whatever he or she is doing and play. Such an adult might feel rejected if the child doesn't want to stop playing with his friends, and therefore may pick him up and move him to a different location to play with the adult-chosen toys (intrusive behavior).

- *Issues about control in the family who raised us.*
  An adult may over-control because he or she was controlled in an authoritarian way in the family in which he or she was raised. Such forcing of a child, as in "you must clean your plate," can eventually lead to eating disorders in children and adolescents. Such adult behavior can stem from the belief that children need to be told and controlled on many matters, rather than simply trusted to be an autonomous individual who can share in decision making with the adult. Similar power struggles can occur around sleeping or any matter. Such power struggles often resolve when children are given some control.

■ *Achievement, overachievement, or perfectionistic needs.*
Sometimes adults, be it parent or teacher or other adult, can push too hard due to their own agendas. An individual might expect a child to do everything one particular way, rather than following the child's lead. Inside, such individuals might be feeling that they know better and can give a head start. Many biological, adoptive, or foster parents say that they feel they are not being good in their role unless they interact and teach something with their child all the time. Some caregivers at child care also feel that they are being paid and should be earning their keep and try to force learning. Of course, some adults are rarely involved and that is not helpful either. The key is to use the language of love—keep the connection, take note of the child's response, and stay involved without doing too much for the child that the child can do on his or her own. Teaching—while maintaining the emotional connection—is the very best scenario.

Optimal nonintrusiveness is an important aspect of the universal language of love because it is in this way that the individual gives space to the child. It is important to remember that intrusiveness is determined not solely by the adult's actions, but also by the child's response to these efforts. One child's fun roughhousing is another child's over-stimulation. It all depends on the response of your child. If a child has disabilities, he or she may appreciate more involvement and directiveness in specific areas (e.g., motor activities) and such adult behavior may not be perceived as taking over. However, for a child who is at ease in those motor activities, an adult's directions may seem intrusive, and the child will let the adult know, in words or deeds, subtly or blatantly.

> **Caring a great deal can lead to intrusive behaviors.**

Behaviors such as wanting the child to eat enough or wanting the child to do well in homework are benign but can "feel" intrusive to the child. What, then, does the wise adult do?

■ Just like all aspects of the language of love, intrusiveness is not just a quality of the adult but a quality of the relationship. What might feel intrusive in one relationship may seem like true caring in another relationship. If you are feeling, or you are made to feel, intrusive, ask yourself if this child has shut you out in any way. If so, you might intuitively feel that you are being intrusive because the relationship has become less of a two-way street. It is then necessary to bring things back to a nonintrusive form; sometimes just the recognition of your intrusiveness can do the trick. I want you now to consider the difference between these two interactions.

> One mom in our research said, "Kiss me," and her 3-year-old began to blow kisses to her and to the others in the living room. Another mom in our research said, "Kiss me" and her toddler began to run away, and she continued to run after him, saying, "I need a kiss," "Give me a kiss."

- Being overly forceful about most things is rarely the answer. For example, force feeding is rarely the answer to eating difficulties with babies (or older children) and can often exacerbate the problem. The soundest advice, given by pediatricians, is to have food available, but not control, let alone over-control, its intake. Power struggles rarely help.

- Power struggles also rarely help in the area of peers. Having dialogues and coaching is different from intrusive lectures about the topic of "that crowd."

- "Be there." At some points in development, particularly in adolescence, just being a physically available, nonintrusive presence can be what a child needs. We adults can respond and interact when we are "invited" to join—such "being there" or "being available" is very reassuring, not intrusive, to children and adolescents. For example, when a parent is driving a child to soccer practice, it might seem less intrusive to talk about "that crowd" than if you sat your child down for a serious talk. A child care professional "being there" in the backyard with all the children, but letting the children congregate around the sandbox may be just what is needed for a perfect outing!

- Sometimes, you might feel so strongly about a particular area (e.g., a particular group of friends, use of certain Internet sites, or another subject) that you *do* want to be intrusive and want to go on record for that. If you have been speaking the universal language of love all along with a child, be it your child or a child you are caring for in child care, or you are a teacher, or other, you can be very direct and open(!), and such direct openness will be heard because you have maintained an emotional connection all along.

# 4. Is There Any Overt or Covert Hostility Present?

Our research indicates that 20 to 30 percent of parents show some degree of hostility (irritability, bad words, and the like) toward their babies and/or young children. Not surprisingly, these percentages are higher as children move toward adolescence. The percentage is also higher with nonparental professional caregivers in a multiple caregiving situation, but may be more veiled, such as shows of boredom or discontent rather than overt or obvious hostility.

It is normal to feel some degree of irritation or anger toward a child every now and then, of course. Being completely responsible for the well-being of a tiny, helpless human being, not to mention caring for groups of children, is sometimes exhausting, frustrating, and maddening. We, however, being older and wiser, can and should keep ourselves from projecting those emotions on or toward the children we love. Adults need to find ways to regulate their negative emotions so that children do not feel like the targets or the sources of stress. During stressful life circumstances, it is difficult to always be upbeat, but it is important for children to see that we can regulate the negative stressors and that overcoming stress can also be valuable.

Significant adults, particularly the parents, parent figures, or other attachment figures, are seen by children as their primary source for everything—food, security, love, health, and so on. When a primary or significant individual takes out his or her feelings on a child, that child's very foundation can be threatened.

The topic of yelling or screaming is worth mentioning. Such outbursts can be just as scary and humiliating for a child as physical abuse. Apologizing as quickly as possible is not a complete remedy, but nevertheless should be done to show respect for the child. Working on the connections between how you were treated when you were a child and your perceptions of this child can make a clear difference.

> One mother who was generally very sensitive and caring told me that she had worked on many issues related to the emotional unavailability of her own mother, but when she began to grow tired or stressed, she "became her yelling mother."

Stress often makes us show the very things we wanted to change about ourselves and it can also be a valuable time to show ourselves that we have overcome any negative attributes left from our childhoods.

Research has indicated that when children hear yelling, they become energized and frenetic in their activity. Much of the yelling or intrusiveness delivered by an adult is meant to stop unwanted child behavior, yet such hostility fuels the very aggressive and overly active behaviors it is supposedly designed to stop—because when there is yelling, the child hears the negative energy but cannot process the words.

> ## If you yell, "Don't do that!" a child likely hears the negative energy and little of the content.

Recently, Bob has been going through a very stressful time. He was laid off from his job and had to take a different position at a lower salary. He now has to work much longer hours. Having grown up with an abusive father, however, he is completely committed never to let his own negative emotions affect his relationship with his family. So Bob has developed several strategies to help him leave his troubles behind when he comes home. Bob uses the drive between the office and home as his chance to unwind. He plays jazz, which he loves, on the car stereo, and he makes a conscious effort to put any bad moments of the day out of his mind. Bob has also set up a signal system with his kids. If the day has gone well and he is in a good place, when he walks in the door he calls, "Where are my red Indians?" That means he's ready for anything—his two sons (ages 7 and 9) can tackle him, tell him about their day, ask for help with homework, and so on. If, however, Bob walks in and says nothing, the kids know he still needs a little space and time to unwind. Most of the time, the kids will wait a while until Bob has had a chance to hang up his coat, put his feet up, and maybe spend a while talking with his wife about what's bothering him. But Bob has an agreement with himself that no matter what, he'll come to the dinner table in as good a mood as he can. His kids feel supported emotionally because they know how important they are to their father and that even though he is going through some rough times, his negative emotions are not directed at them.

Often individuals think they are "keeping the lid on" their negative emotions, but unless they can process and handle such emotions, there is a tendency for them to "leak." This leakage usually creates covert rather than overt hostility. Signs that a child may read as covert hostility include a slightly raised voice, boredom, impatience, and so on. This can progress to, for example, resentment, "huffing and puffing," rolling your eyes, teasing with an edge, raising your voice, being easily irritated, or showing a long-suffering attitude. Covert hostility can produce passive-aggressive behaviors, or cause an individual to disconnect from the very people he or she most loves. Therefore, we must all be wary and deal with negative emotions by all means available (psychotherapy, talking to a spouse or good friend, introspection) to prevent their impact on the next generation.

Leaks of covert hostility can be detrimental to a child. Our research involves going into people's homes and videotaping parent-child interactions for an hour or more per session. For obvious reasons, we usually don't see overt signs of hostility, such as yelling or hitting, during our time in the home. But we do see low levels of covert hostility, such as rolling the eyes or making a sarcastic comment ("What a mess you made," or "What a dirty little girl you are"). We see the same thing in classroom settings. A parent might go into the school classroom and compliment the child on a picture well done and then turn to the teacher (within earshot of the child) and say, "What is it?" (with a laugh). These are leaks of covert hostility, and they signal to the child that the parent has some negative feelings toward him or her.

In its most pronounced form, hostility becomes overt. Adults become overly harsh, abrasive, and demeaning, either facially or vocally or both. They may threaten and/or frighten, with teasing, shaming, ridiculing, and so on. Sometimes the threats may be in the form of a joke ("I'll send you to an orphanage if you keep that up"), but children take such threats of separation or abandonment very seriously. In some circumstances, the hostility is not directed at the child but is a significant part of the child's environment. An adult who habitually loses his or her temper and yells at anyone and anything, for example, would be demonstrating overt hostility, even though it might not be directed toward the child. Unfortunately, for their health and sense of security, children are very emotionally attuned as a rule.

> **When they are young, children cannot differentiate between hostility directed toward someone else and hostility directed toward them. Cognitively, they feel that they are at the center and have caused the negative emotions in the household.**

I have seen many adults who show a capacity for sensitivity, but who also "fly off the handle" easily. Caregiving is not about sainthood. All children push buttons sometimes, and all adults push buttons as well. But, as a caregiver, one of the most important "lessons" one can teach is how, in regular, day-to-day life, to regulate emotions when the going gets rough. The rough day at the child care site when many children are sick or the rough time at home just as the family is getting back home after a long day are the most telling times for "teaching" about the language of love. We find that we often cannot see hostility in our research unless we set up such stressful situations.

- When the adult is tired, or stressed, or pushed and pulled in different directions, the adult is at risk of "losing cool." After making sure that a child (or the children) is safe (e.g., not in the bathtub or on a changing table), taking a time out is the cool thing to do.

> **It is curious that the language of love becomes even more important during the stressful times, during times of fatigue, and during times when we may not be at our best.**

- If you have crossed this boundary, do apologize. Adults do make mistakes and children can see that correcting mistakes is possible. Restore justice and fairness by an apology—relationships should be just and fair, not angry and unfair.

> **Many adults mistakenly feel that they have privileges that children do not have—and that their own behavior is not the point.**

- Through nonhostile, peaceful, just, and fair interactions, adults teach about the language of relationships—how good relationships should feel. When a significant adult or parent (or parent figure) is covertly hostile, impatient, shaming, or putting others down, that individual is bullying, and a child is learning an important negative lesson: that he or she can be bullied by others in relationships and that he or she can do the same to others. More obvious lessons about violence, the permission for violence, and the like are learned in overtly hostile relationships. Children carry these templates into their other relationships.

> A third-grader once told me, "My mom threw this paperback at me in the kitchen." He was also a child who showed aggressive displays with peers on the playground. His behavior spoke volumes about what goes on at home regularly, even though when mom came to pick him up at school, she was always "all smiles" and very (apparently) pleasant with everyone. Most of the important lessons we all teach our children occur when we are least aware that we are "on stage."

■ Some individuals see covert (or overt) hostility in their own behavior and feel badly that they have "stepped over the line." They seem conscious of some of these behaviors and catch themselves. Many others, however, are less aware that they step over the line. For example, many adults use threats but don't ever carry out such threats—they don't even have any intention to.

> **Nonetheless, threats of violence ("if you do that again, I will throw you against that wall"), threats of separation ("I'm going to leave you kids if you do that"), threats of loss ("I'll kill myself")—are as real to a child as the action.**

Such threats are frightening to a child. Often, such threats are said in a joking way, but the universal language of love is such that children are either confused by the lack of congruence in verbal/nonverbal channels or they often believe what is said to them.

> One father said of his son, "He only remembers all the things I did wrong, but I also did so much for him." This father was right. Hostility is remembered—not necessarily at a conscious, mental level, but at the level of feelings. Memory is not objective; it is emotional. To build positive emotional memories, you must unload stress, think positive thoughts, relax as much as

you can, take time outs, find supportive networks of friends and family (parents, parent figures, or nonparental professional caregivers all need support!), and especially limit even covert hostility. Children remember about us (and about others) the emotions they feel when they are with us. Consider both of the following scenarios and how these families thought through and worked on their anger.

A divorced father who had just had cancer surgery and had a new bladder (neobladder) lived in a rural area with his two sons and no one nearby for 200 miles. The pain and complications often became unbearable, and he would scream, "I'm going to kill myself if you don't quiet down," or "I can't take it any more." He had wanted no help from anyone. He soon began to realize, however, that the boys needed others and deserved more calm, so he consented to sending them to their mother, at least while he recovered. Although the choice was a hard one for him, he did realize that when the language of love is tainted with so much hostility, it cannot be a good thing for the next generation.

Adam had been in the army for the past year, and when he came back, his son was a year old! It was awesome to meet him for the first time, but Adam also had a lot of adjustment before he could feel comfortable with parenting. He had gone through some really stressful times while away, including sustaining injuries to his face. However, his wife was welcoming both of him and of the chance to have a partner in raising their baby. Nonetheless, they decided that until he could get used to the routines, she would be present and would not leave him "in charge" just yet. They had heard that many veterans coming back from war had difficulty controlling anger, and they wanted to make sure they took it slowly.

## 5. Is This Child Responsive to You?

Once again, we're back to the child's side of the adult-child equation. The components of emotional availability are part of a whole relationship construct, with many different factors interrelating and interacting to form a healthy (or unhealthy) whole. Ultimately, any relationship is about just that: the act of relating to each other. In this ideal adult-child relationship, the adult has the most responsibility and flexibility in creating something that both parties will enjoy. However, the only way to tell whether the relationship is working is to see how the child responds to the adult's attempts to connect emotionally.

In our research, we see a child's responsiveness to the adult reflected in two aspects of the child's behavior. First is the child's eagerness or willingness to engage with the adult when the adult offers a suggestion or moves to interact with the child. What we are looking for is a child who looks up and talks to the adult in an enthusiastic, engaged tone—a child who appears eager to connect with the adult. What is important is not just the response itself, but the emotional quality of the response from the child.

If the child ignores the adult when approached, or generally appears bland or blasé to the overture, then obviously the child is not really emotionally responsive. If the child looks up and talks to the adult but seems unhappy or uses simply an unenthusiastic tone—even if he or she does what the adult asked—that, too, is not being emotionally responsive. In some cases, the child may avoid the gaze of the adult or move away.

Conversely, we have seen situations in which the significant adult doesn't reach out to the child or initiate much contact (the research indicates that in U.S. households, parents speak to children on average 12 minutes per day), and the child continues to play on his or her own. In child care sites, many caregivers balance basic care with solid interactions, but others are so busy making sure that the day-to-day running of a site is going well that they often do not realize that children need to have conversations with adults on some regular basis, and these conversations need to be elaborated and become full of life. We need to all attend to this and make sure the children are getting real emotional food.

An aspect of a child's behavior that indicates lack of optimal responsiveness is what we call a "negative cycle of connectedness." When a child is approached by an adult and, instead of ignoring or avoiding the overture, the child becomes whiny, complains, insults, cries, or appears anxious or fearful, something is obviously wrong. The child is responding negatively to the adult's attempt to connect, and this often indicates a dysfunctional means of maintaining contact.

> Patty was a premature baby, and her lungs were not fully developed. Throughout her infancy she had had trouble with

asthma, bronchitis, and a range of other lung-related problems. Her parents were so concerned about her health that practically every time Patty coughed, they would rush her to the hospital. They found it difficult to relate to their daughter without an overlay of fear and worry. Whenever Patty's parents tried to play with her, Patty would become whiny and push them away. Because of the health problems, the family had created a negative cycle of connectedness, from which they now had to emerge toward a more real and secure emotional connection. But they were not there as yet.

This is not to say that smiling, laughing children are always considered emotionally responsive. Some children will smile and laugh a great deal during a play session, but if the emotion is directed only at the play activities, and it is clear that the child is avoiding the adult by focusing emotion on the imaginary world of play, then it is obvious that the child is not connecting with that adult. Also, some children use nervous, overly bright smiles and laughter as a way of pleasing others, and this style of relating, too, is indicative of an insecure emotional connection with that adult.

Recently, Claudia brought her 1-year-old baby, Sonya, into our clinic. Whenever her mother left the room, even for 10 seconds, Sonya showed extreme distress—full-blown crying and complete unsoothability by anyone else. As soon as Claudia returned, Sonya settled only reluctantly and would not let Claudia out of her sight for the rest of the session. We asked Claudia about their life together, and she said that she had never left Sonya with others, even with grandparents, and that she took the baby with her everywhere. Claudia reported that Sonya showed extreme distress whenever she left her, even for a moment to go to the bathroom. Claudia therefore tried to keep her unavailability to a minimum because it distressed her baby so much. We did talk to her about how she in fact needs to signal her unavailability at times, without breaking the emotional connection, so that Claudia could begin to feel her own power; for example, talking to Claudia to support her at a distance.

Children who are optimally emotionally responsive to a specific significant adult usually demonstrate a happy and content countenance. They are content pursuing autonomous activities but they also respond in a positive way toward that adult at appropriate points. Their response generally shows pleasure and eagerness without any sense of urgency or necessity. They smile or laugh appropriately, and usually attend to adults' comments, questions, suggestions, and demonstrations with ease. Emotionally responsive children may not respond to every request, however, especially when they are engrossed in play. But there is the sense that, for the most part, the child is comfortable with and willing to respond to the overtures in this adult-child relationship.

If the emotional responsiveness is not at the highest level, the child may respond but seem unenthusiastic about doing so. The child may respond slowly and reluctantly, continuing play as if he or she didn't hear the adult. The child who always responds to the adult in an overeager, overly bright way is also not optimal, as described above; this may indicate a reversal in roles (the child feeling like he or she has to take care of the adult, rather than the other way around). In the most serious cases of emotional unresponsiveness, the child's emotional health may be in danger. Here we see the kind of avoidance behaviors described above—ignoring parental requests, turning away from parents, strong protests that appear inappropriate, or affect that is very concerning (e.g., emotional withdrawal, emotional dysregulation, frightened behavior).

When I say "responsiveness," I am not referring simply to the child's compliance with the significant adult's wishes, but to the emotional richness, happiness, and tenderness that is shared between attachment figures. Therefore, the importance of a child's responsiveness cannot be overstressed. This measure is the best clinical criteria for assessing the child's emotional availability to the parent. It is the adult's very best and clearest clue that there is a secure emotional connection. If, on the other hand, the adult feels or senses that a child is not really emotionally responsive, the remedy is to attend to the adult's side of the universal language of love—that is what you can focus on. "Reading" where we are in the relationship is the first step in being able to enhance the relationship without that, we would all be clueless about where we are in our close relationships.

A healthy emotional responsiveness, and how it is nurtured, follows.

> Caroline was concerned about the emotional "health" of her
> baby, Sammy, if she were to do work around the house that did
> not involve him. Caroline sometimes felt guilty about needing
> to clean or do other tasks. She brought these concerns to my
> clinic, where I reassured her: "It's important for babies to be

able to explore independently and experience the world autonomously," I said. "Such explorations occur best in proximity to the parent, certainly. But in a healthy emotional relationship, the presence of a parent can trigger a child's need to move out into the world. Children will explore other areas of the house in a way they would not think of unless a parent was readily—although not completely—available." I recommended that Caroline experiment with encouraging Sammy to explore while she did housework near him.

Caroline later came back and told me her guilt had vanished. She discovered that if she established a nice emotional connection with Sammy and then set him up with some toys, she felt comfortable about taking care of her work and he felt comfortable about exploring his world of toys on his own. Both mother and son reconnected frequently as they both "worked," and those reconnections would reconfirm their emotional tie. The cycle of "moving out" and then "moving back together" would start again.

Caroline's experience describes perfectly the kind of relationship an emotionally available mother and baby share.

Being constantly available is not good for creating healthy emotional availability. Of course, I don't mean that you should take off for a month's vacation and leave your new baby at home! However, babies need to explore the world on their own, with parents available for monitoring should it be needed. In this way, your baby feels your presence, garnering a sense of safety and security, but also senses that you have other tasks, and that doing them with gusto is important to you.

> ## How can you tell if a child is responsive to you in the context of your relationship?

- Remember, responsiveness is not obedience or compliance. It is emotional responsiveness toward you, with a balance between connection with you and explorations away from you. A child who shows positive responsiveness toward a significant adult is likely to be secure with that adult. So, go on and observe whether this child is responsive to you—seeming generally happy and content in his or her life and showing a balance between "moving away" and "moving toward" you.

- Some children are emotionally responsive, but show many signs of distress, such as whining and the like. These children have become accustomed to drawing people in through negative cycles of relatedness, as we discussed earlier in this chapter. They have learned that if they are distressed, they will receive caring, and if they whine, someone will come to soothe them. Many of these children engage in dependent interactions with their teachers as well, staying near the teacher and being comforted by adults. Rather than engage in catering behavior that would encourage and prolong this type of responsiveness (an unhealthy kind), trust this child to grow emotionally, and subtly and kindly demand more mature emotional responses. If you are the child care professional, preschool teacher, or elementary/middle school teacher, you can empower this type of child to grow stronger and taller by trusting him or her to take on more responsibility that perhaps has been given to that child in the past. Giving more space and more responsibility can do wonders for this type of child. If you are the biological parent, and you have taken on too much responsibility (perhaps because of prematurity, illness, or other fears of losing this child), you can begin to change the dynamics of this relationship. As you change the ground rules, take note of how your child might rise to this new and promising challenge of autonomy. If you are the foster or adoptive parent, ponder what might have made this child so clingy, whiny, and dependent. You can simultaneously set the stage for a new style of relatedness with the child, one with which he or she may not at first feel familiar, but over time, you can set new ground rules and ones that are communicating a new love language based on the science of emotional availability.

- Many children show pleasing behaviors toward parents and/or others, as if they are engaging in caregiving or parenting behaviors with the adult. If such a pattern of pseudoforms of mature behavior is going on, again let this child know that he or she does not need to "take care of others"—that he or she is the "kid." We have seen such behavior in children when a parent in the home has been depressed or traumatized; the children then take it upon themselves to "make things right." Obviously, such behavior is burdensome for the child and can be framed into a more positive and healthy direction. Play with such a child, and in the context of play, you can show that the child does not need to be the pleaser all the time; he or she can also be the one pleased and the one heard.

- Some children seem avoidant and unresponsive. If during play or otherwise, the child seems not to "return the serve," then try *not* to keep "hitting the ball." Instead, wait for the child to come to you, and then elaborate and show pleasure in positive sharing of emotions together. With consistent availability and emotional responsiveness on your part, this seemingly unresponsive child will begin to learn a new language of relationships and will likely become less avoidant and unresponsive over time. Many children (especially foster and adopted children) have become so unresponsive and avoidant over time that it is a challenge to win them over. The same strategies can work with them, except that the foster or adoptive parent needs to know that he or she is "in it for the long haul." Progress can be met by several steps back in such relationships. The idea is to maintain the trust and consistency and to "surprise" such a child about relationships by not giving up in the face of such challenges. Consistent care can create change!

But what if you are constantly being separated from your child, such as when you are in the military or for other reasons?

> Harry, an active-duty marine, and Terri had one daughter together and she had two other older children from a prior relationship. Harry was thrilled to be a dad and they knew that Lela would be their last child. Due to his military career, however, Harry had been deployed twice during the lifetime of their daughter, so he had been able to see her for only very brief periods of time. When he was home, Terri was always thrilled to have him back, but Lela would not seek him out and would often treat him as if she barely knew him. During one return to San Diego, they decided that it would be good for just father and daughter to take a vacation together for a week, but Lela was "frozen" and avoidant of her father. Soon, Terri, the principal attachment figure, joined them. Slowly, Lela began to warm up to her dad and would sit on his lap in a cautious way, but only when Terri was available. They had realized that it's not possible to hurry the expressions of love from a child and that Harry would need to slowly invest in this father-child relationship and invest while physically present (by using all six aspects of the language of love). When he was not physically present, Harry would have to work to express these aspects of the language of love at a distance, through webcam,

through email, through videotapes of him reading stories at night, through photos, and through presents sent just at the right times, such as birthdays or at special events. When Harry began to understand that Lela loved him, but avoided him because she herself feared repeated rejection and abandonment, he began to invest in these different ways, and began to see the beginnings of attachment bonds. Understanding the language of love Lela was expressing (unconsciously, of course) really helped him to respond in a productive and positive way.

## 6. Does This Child Allow You to Be Involved in His or Her Life?

This is a measurement that will gain in importance as your child grows and matures. Parents usually must be totally involved with babies' lives simply because babies are dependent on their first caregivers. But as a baby grows, goes to child care, then preschool, then elementary school, then middle school, high school, and beyond, the child will be the one who decides just how much and to what extent the emotional relationship can grow. Healthy emotional access and involvement are the last key components of emotional availability.

When we assess involvement in a clinical setting, we look at the degree to which the child attends to and engages the adult in play. Typically, children will either make adults the audience for their activities or engage them as playmates or support people. Asking questions, narrating a story line, requesting assistance, or demonstrating materials to adults are all examples of involving behavior. Sometimes children will involve adults simply by looking toward them. A healthy caregiver-child relationship has a balance between autonomous play and requests for adult involvement. The child appears eager (anticipatory) but not anxious as he or she tries to engage the adult. The relationship is a comfortable, positive one for both adult and child.

At lower levels of involvement, children show more interest in the task at hand than in engaging adults' attention. It seems that these children are more oriented toward solitary play, with occasional reference to the significant attachment figures in their lives. Adults appear more like tools the children use when needed, rather than a desired audience. As the amount of involvement decreases, these children may avoid their significant caregivers altogether, literally turning their backs on them. At the most severe levels of uninvolvement, children do not seek to involve caregivers at all. If caregivers try to engage the children, there may be some response, but the children make no attempt to elaborate on the exchange and do not initiate new ones. It is as if the children are completely uninterested in the caregivers. Or the opposite may occur: the children may over-involve the caregivers, insisting they cannot play by themselves, offering toys, and constantly speaking to, looking at, or seeking physical contact from them. These actions may be accompanied by anxiety, whining, "acting out," complaining, and other forms of negative emotional expression.

Of course, many children will show a range of involvement, depending on their mood, but here we are talking about what things *usually* are like. Here, it's important to state that the same children may show different qualities of the language of love with different caregivers; in particular, during infancy. Science indicates that at least during the infancy period (the first two years of life), children have a tendency to keep relationships separate in some way, when those relationships are measured under very controlled experimental conditions, but there is also indication that at all ages and stages, children can also show carryover from one relationship of love to another relationship of love.

One of the ways we measure a child's involvement with the attachment figure is through "storytelling talks." We meet with the child separately and ask him or her to tell a story about his or her parents. Often, uninvolved children will tell stories about being angry with their parents, or stories in which they are hurt and their parents don't comfort them. Conversely, children who enjoy involvement with their parents will relate incidents in which their parents took care of them, or about going on outings or adventures with their parents, or perhaps about going on adventures by themselves and being warmly welcomed by their parents when they returned. What follows are two very different types of real stories from our research files, the first with a very different language of love than the second.

> Three-year-old Thomas was enacting a story about his mother and father going on a vacation. He "drove" the family car away. He and his older sister, Marie, were staying behind with the babysitter. He described how much fun they were going to have watching TV and eating lots and lots of popcorn. "And soon," he said, "mommy and daddy will be coming back with t-shirts for each of them."

In contrast, three-year-old Danny pushed the car (and the mommy and daddy in the car) off the table, saying, "We need to get rid of them!" He then proceeded to watch TV with the babysitter.

The highest compliment a child can pay to you as the adult is the desire to involve you in his or her play, problems, school, and life. Healthy levels of involvement mean that you have earned the love and trust of this child. It is one of the last, best measures of the success of your efforts to create a strong and supportive adult-child connection.

A little girl, Sherrie, was in the community swimming pool area with her grandpa. He, however, was focused on his newspaper. By the time he paid attention to her—when the child was hurt—the little girl no longer responded to him. Her level of emotional responsiveness had decreased because her grandfather had not responded to her earlier when she was looking up, smiling, hollering across the pool to play ball with him. He normally paid a great deal of attention to her, which is why she had been so persistent in involving him earlier.

Healthy levels of involvement should not be confused with children who become fast friends with strangers at the supermarket and who immediately involve them in their lives, or children who are emotionally or physically abused and/or neglected and cling and try to please their perpetrators so that they are not further harmed. Such adult-child relationships are dysfunctional and a distortion of the language of love, and in all these painful life conditions, child affect is the key. Children who are emotionally available in a healthy way are robust, purposeful, calm, and content, in contrast to the distressed, over-pleasing, frightened, or frightening way in which dysfunctional life scenarios can distort a child's language of love.

Angie was 18 months old and being observed at a university-based child care site by a psychology research intern. The intern was taking notes on everything about this little girl, and of course, looking at her fairly regularly. Angie quickly showed rapt attention to the observer and began to climb on her. As the observer would move away, Angie would follow and continue clinging, which made writing almost impossible.

This is an over-involving type of interaction, based on indiscriminate sociability, and certainly not what we mean by optimal involvement.

> ### If a child is responsive to you, the child is also likely to be involving you in his or her life.

But, take note—is it involvement in positive or less positive ways?

When a child runs up to his or her mother to tell her something as they are about to leave the school, and gives her a kiss, that's child involvement! It's important to recognize involvement when you see it! Much of emotional availability or emotional unavailability is not only about our side of the equation, but also about recognizing the other side of the equation when we see it.

In one of our research programs to improve emotional availability in our community, we went to child care sites and enlisted the help of child care providers. We went to sites serving lower-income as well as higher-income families. Our funding source, fortunately, did not limit our work to only lower-income families because all children need the skills of emotional availability. In one site, the child care professionals described 2-year-old Jimmy, who did not have any friends and who did not ask much of anyone. The parents, both doctors, were very emotionally unavailable to him, and in the two years that he had been at the center, the professionals had not met the mother or father because Jimmy was always brought to the center and picked up by the nanny. In fact, the nanny went to their house quite early in the morning so that she could get him ready, while the parents slept in a little later. On weekends, the nanny was again at their house so that the family could entertain and Jimmy could be kept away from the entertainment area. Over the course of the program, in which we coached child care professionals on working to improve children's attachments and skills in this area, Jimmy became much more interactive both with the professionals and with his age-mates, and apparently also with his parents. In fact, he demanded a back rub each evening before bed and would not sleep until he was soothed in this way. The parents, however, did not recognize this lovely sign of involvement from Jimmy, his desire to involve them in this life, and made a special trip to the child care site to complain about his behavior at home.

It was obviously difficult for these parents to understand their child's cues and communications. This vignette (from our research files) indicates that it may be a good idea to require parent participation in social programs such as the one described above—perhaps through tax breaks or other small incentives—to coach parents about the universal language of love. Then a cycle of avoidance and unresponsiveness would not be seen as the norm, and signs of real love could be recognized and elaborated. Conversely, negative forms of child involvement are obviously not optimal and are measured low on our test. They are a child's cries for help. For example, if a child has started bullying other children at school and the parents are getting regular phone calls from the teacher or principal, that's also child involvement, but of the negative kind, which would be scored low on our test. Children don't know how to describe that they are feeling depressed or rejected or angry, and thus they "act out."

Of course, in real life, the six elements of emotional availability are not separate at all—they are interrelated in complex ways. Best of all, most of the time we connect emotionally with our child or children or the children we teach without having to think about it. It's kind of like sailing a boat. You can study nautical theory and the dynamics of wind and waves, and this knowledge can help you figure out what to do on a boat, but when you're out at sea, with waves hitting the sides of the boat and the sail flapping in the wind, you don't stop to think, "How much air pressure does that sail need to get me across the lake?" You let the knowledge you've studied and absorbed help you as you make the split-second decisions required by the circumstances of the moment. This knowledge about where your relationships are with children (one relationship at a time!) really can help you in those split-second emotional decisions.

## Creating a Whole from the Parts of the Language of Love

Let's look at an example of child behavior and adult behavior, and bring in the adult's perceptions about nature versus nurture in a child who is sensitive "by birth."

> Maria brought her 2-year-old son, Carl, to see me at our clinic. She told me that Carl was born shy, sensitive, and even hypersensitive. "He cries all the time," Maria said. "He won't

respond to anyone he doesn't know. He's not outgoing with other children. I don't know what's wrong with him." From the way Maria talked about her child, it was clear that she saw Carl's temperament and general lack of boldness as negative or weak. (This kind of response may arise when the mother is of the same temperament and was not treated in a sensitive manner during her own childhood development, or for other reasons.)

Maria tended to respond to Carl's crying or fear by deriding him, telling him to "be a little man," or by ignoring his emotional distress. She seemed somewhat hostile and impatient; rather than empowering Carl or strengthening his sense of confidence, she "talked down" to him. When Carl was unwilling to explore his environment on his own, Maria became intrusive, trying to "make" Carl try out a new toy. When asked about her behavior, Maria said, "I have to be hard on him or he won't ever try anything new."

Maria viewed Carl as difficult to be with, both for her and for other children. As a result, she didn't pay much attention to structuring his play time, delivering well-timed or well-appointed suggestions about how to play, or setting up playdates with other children. Unfortunately, Maria's perception of Carl and her resulting behavior caused Carl to develop a kind of shell, an armor. He became less responsive to Maria, and less willing to attempt to include her in his play. He also shut himself off from others.

When a parent's perceptions do not allow a child to learn new ways of relating to others and to the world, such perceptions can become a self-fulfilling prophecy. Maria's behavior was not leading to an emotionally close relationship with her son. Let us look at Maria's actions in view of the six elements of emotional availability. Because Maria viewed Carl's sensitivity as a problem or weakness, she responded negatively to his attempts to recruit her emotionally, telling him to "be a little man" rather than picking him up or reassuring him. As a result, Carl stopped responding to his mother's emotional overtures (element #5). When Carl stopped responding to her, Maria's sensitivity to his needs decreased (element #1). She also became more hostile (element #4), demanding that Carl stop being so afraid and trying to force and intrude upon him to try new things (element #3) and over-structuring his play (element #2). But Carl refused to respond to Maria's demands (element #5) and began ignoring her and starting to cry even harder (element #6).

Fortunately, parents can change their level of emotional availability/unavailability fairly easily, beginning with changing their view of the child's inborn nature. When parents change their view of and their behavior toward their child, the child's view of the parent can change as well.

> I suggested to Maria that she change her view of Carl's sensitivity and regard the trait either as positive or, at the very least, neutral. "You're communicating to Carl that something's wrong with him," I said. "And no one wants to feel that there's something wrong with who they are."
>
> If she regarded Carl's sensitivity in a positive light, I told Maria, she would find that he would respond quickly and positively to her encouragement and that he would interact more boldly with his environment. "Positive attributions about our children can have powerful effects on them and on us," I said. I then confided to Maria, "When my daughter was born, she cried nonstop for four months. While I was soothing her, I sang her songs I made up about how easy she was and how fun everything was around our house." (I sing some of those songs around our house to this day—they still make us laugh.) I reminded Maria that sensitive children respond very well to their caregiver's shaping, so in those terms, Carl's sensitivity would make her job as a parent easier.
>
> For the next few weeks Maria and Carl came to the clinic for observation and coaching. Maria learned how to encourage Carl whenever he attempted something new or exhibited a little more boldness. She also became more nonintrusive in Carl's play, allowing him to explore his environment in his own time and on his own terms, and praising him when he did so. She made a point of being patient with Carl's difficulties, supporting him to learn on his own and thus creating greater self-confidence in him. Outside of the clinic environment, Maria set up playdates for Carl with other toddlers, allowing her son to have more experience with his peers without her constant supervision. I encouraged Maria to enroll Carl in a nursery school for a few mornings a week, to give him an opportunity

to develop without any (potential) overprotection on her part. (There is evidence that when parents provide more social opportunities for shy or sensitive children, the children often grow out of shyness.)

Carl responded to Maria's new style of nurturing with more openness to his mother's interactions. As he was allowed to explore on his own, and was genuinely praised for every small increase in confidence, he began to enjoy more creative and challenging play. He also became more open with other children. Carl was still sensitive and a little fearful when presented with new people and situations, but he quickly overcame his shyness with a little reassurance from his mother or a little time to explore new situations on his own. Because children are able to get over their inborn shyness, it is likely that shyness to a good extent can be overcome with nurture.

Our positive perceptions of our children can have an immediate and long-lasting effect on our children's self-esteem. Evidence by Susan Campbell at the University of Pittsburgh shows that positive perceptions can have a life of their own. One very interesting study evaluated both a baby's temperament and the parent's perception of the baby's temperament. Researchers observed young babies and objectively evaluated their temperaments on a scale from easy to difficult. Each parent was then asked to rate his or her baby's temperament on the same scale. Many months later, the babies were reevaluated on the same temperament scale. Researchers found that a parent's positive perception of the child's temperament had a positive effect on the child over time. Children who were assessed originally as difficult (based on the researchers' objective observations) but whose parents viewed them as easygoing were measured as much easier in temperament (judged again by objective observations) when they were older.

This effect that parents have on a child's emotional responsiveness demonstrates one of the fundamental rewards for a parent's positive perceptions: *our children become more responsive to us.* Children are responsive to parents who try to establish a healthy connection with them. Certainly, a child's level of emotional responsiveness is affected by its inborn nature, but I would rate nature as only 20 percent of the equation. The other 80 percent of emotional responsiveness has to do with what the child feels is coming (or not coming) from the parent. As the adult, you are the one who is supposed to have some control over your behavior and your emotions.

As a parent, it is your responsibility to set up a climate of healthy, available emotional connection with your child.

# A Note on Emotional Availability as Being "Good at Repairs"

In the early days of research into emotional availability, investigators described qualities such as sensitivity as an almost "exquisite responsiveness." Sensitivity was described in all-positive terms, and only beautiful qualities were included in this concept, such as clearly perceiving an individual's needs, promptly responding to signals and communications, being aware of a sense of timing, and so on. A mother was supposed to "sense" her baby's needs the instant the child emerged from her womb. Likewise, an adult was supposed to "sense" what a significant other adult was thinking.[1]

However, as any mother or father will tell you, nothing could be further from the truth. Parenting is a process of trial and error, with the emphasis on error. Children have different needs, and even if you are the most experienced parent in the world, what worked with your firstborn probably won't work with your second—especially when it comes to emotional needs. Emotional availability is not "perfect parenting." In fact, emotional availability acknowledges the importance of the parent's ability to consistently "repair" the relationship with the child after conflicts. It is much more realistic to look at emotional availability as being "good at repairs" rather than being "perfect."

This need for relationship repair is apparent even with babies as young as 6 months of age. One study analyzed moment-to-moment interactions between mothers and their babies during playtimes. It showed that 50 percent of the exchanges between mother and child were nonsynchronous— meaning that there were consistent conflicts or emotional "bumps" in the parent-child relationship. This suggests that repairing our relationships with our children is a normal aspect of emotional availability. Many of us recognize the need for relationship repair with our older children, but we are less aware of doing this with our babies. Even during play, if we look at moment-to-moment exchanges, we are consistently repairing our relation-

---

[1] Surely, adult-adult interactions are about repairs and the capacity and caring enough to repair. Astute leaders are also good at repair, not seemingly omniscient and omnipotent, the topic of the last chapter.

ships to move our children out of conflict and into a more harmonious emotional state.

Note, with respect to the child scales, if your young child is not responsive to and/or involving you, please make sure to get professional advice.

> Parents and caregivers often have good hunches about disorders, including but not limited to autism spectrum disorder, where children have difficulty with social interactions. Such conditions should be checked out by professionals. When caught earlier rather than later, excellent social interventions can be effectively implemented—but seeking professional help and advice is necessary.

And, now here is a way you can check up on your own emotional availability—informally, that is. Know that this is not the full instrument but a brief version that will give you an idea of how you are doing. It is a "look into the kitchen" and is not the full scientific measurement, but you can use it to get a general and informal idea of how you are doing. Good scientists would never think of using the unvalidated, brief form, but it certainly is a place to informally start.

# 3 Emotional Availability/Unavailability Tests

This chapter presents non-research-based versions of the emotional availability tests.[1] Please know that these tests are presented here to give you a ballpark idea of how your check-up is going and, thus, can serve as a rough guide for your *personal* use. The author does not give professionals permission to use these tests to evaluate in any type of *professional* capacity--they are solely for your personal use. Please write to the author at www.emotionalavailability.com for the research-based versions and for permission to use the system, which all require training.

The EA scales consist of six dimensions of the emotional availability of an adult toward a child and of the child toward the adult. The adult dimensions are sensitivity, structuring, nonintrusiveness, and nonhostility, and the child dimensions are the child's responsiveness to the adult and the child's involvement of the parent.

Several general but significant points must be made about the emotional availability framework. First, observation of an interaction via the EA framework requires a sensitivity about context. In contrast to approaches using counts of discrete behaviors, EA is a global or holistic judgment by which the observer uses contextual cues and clinical judgment to infer the appropriateness of behaviors. Second, clinical sensitivity of the observer to emotional cues is key. Here we refer not only to the emotional signaling of the adult to the child but also the signaling of the child to the adult. For example, an adult who is behaviorally doing all the right things but is not emotionally present for the child and/or does not appear to receive the child's emotional signaling (including the absence of emotional displays) cannot be viewed as highly sensitive. Emotional signaling is important for all the dimensions of EA. Third, we view all EA dimensions as relationship variables. For example, a given adult is sensitive within the context of a particular relationship. Thus, we do not believe it accurate to make judgments about a "core" or "trait" of emotional availability, but prefer to view this construct as indexed by particular styles in a relationship context. What the range of a particular individual's emotional availability (in the context of different relationships) might be is an interesting research question that remains to be explored.

For each of the dimensions of emotional availability (caregiver sensitivity, structuring, nonintrusiveness, and nonhostility, and child responsiveness and child involvement), shown below, rate the quality of a "target" relationship. For example, if you are rating yourself, pick a specific child in your family, a specific child in your child care site, or a specific child in the context of your life, and rate each of these dimensions by "observing your relationship." If instead you are rating someone else's relationship with a child, again rate that relationship by "observing it." Observing refers to your filming or directly observing that particular relationship for 20 to 30 minutes (by taking notes) and than deciding which rating best described the target relationship.

Scores on the following scales that are generally on the high end indicate that the relationship has a "clean bill of health." *The attachment relationship is secure and solid!* It does not mean that the relationship is "perfect"—just that it has helped to create emotional security in the child. The mid-range indicates clear inconsistencies, questions, and doubts about this relationship. Generally low scores suggest that the relationship is *insecure in a cool, detached, avoidant way*. A cluster of very low ratings on some or many scales suggests that the relationship is *extremely problematic* and may even be traumatized (e.g., the child may be abused or neglected by someone). A caregiver-child relationship (e.g., child care professional with a target child in a center-based care) may look insecure if a child has had difficult relationships with an attachment figure or someone else, but it does not mean that the particular caregiver being observed is "responsible" for the difficulties, as children bring their entire histories into important relationships. However, any caregiver can be part of the solution of moving a child toward secure attachments!

An extra note should be made here concerning the dimension of sensitivity score in the mid-range. The adult is actually *apparently* sensitive but not really so (looks that way in many ways but is not creating a secure relationship, most likely because the relationship is over-connected rather than secure and appropriately connected). This distinction is crucial: Many over-connected relationships (which are not good for a child) can look pleasant, but the over-connection undermines a child's sense of growth and individuality.

Three different types of inconsistencies in interaction are often missed. Such interactions are often viewed by investigators as highly sensitive, when in fact they should be viewed as "apparently sensitive," or the mid-range. The first two types refer to inconsistencies inherent in the adult's behavior.

- The first type is the inconsistency between declarative knowledge and emotional/affective procedures. This inconsistency typically takes the form of an adult having enough knowledge about how to be sensitive that he or she can almost appear that way. At the declarative level, this adult tries different things to keep the child's attention, appears positively attentive, and often may be very accommodating. What belies this surface sensitivity is *affect*—which might be bland, flat, sugary sweet, pretentious, labile, anxious, hyperexaggerated, or hyperexcitable.

- The second type of inconsistency that resides within the adult occurs when the adult is warm but fails to do what is ultimately good for the affective development of the child. Although this behavior is much more optimal than a cool, detached stance toward the child, warmth is not synonymous with sensitivity. It is a component of it. Affective warmth is necessary for a high rating but it is not sufficient to get a high rating. Adult warmth may be coupled with other qualities such as (a) infantilization (i.e., treating the child as much younger than the child actually is or doing things for the child that the child can do for himself or herself) or (b) other subtle forms or strategies to control the behavior of the child. These combined qualities of adult warmth with controlling or infantilizing strategies may lead to parent-child *fusion or enmeshment.*

- The third type of inconsistent sensitivity refers to inconsistency within the adult-child dyad. Because a highly sensitive adult has a keen sense of what optimal adult-child interactions *feel* like for the interactants, sustained unresponsiveness by the child would be emotionally received by the adult and alternative strategies would be pursued. *Thus, a highly sensitive adult would not engage in an interactional style that is one-sided.*

> These scales should be used when you have a chance to actually *observe* for about 20 to 30 minutes.

## Adult Sensitivity

5     *Highly sensitive.* Highly sensitive. Emotional communication between the adult and child for the most part is positive, appropriate, and creative. The highly sensitive adult displays much genuine, authentic, and congruent interest, pleasure, and amusement with the child (as opposed to performing these behaviors), as demonstrated by warm smiles and giggles, interested eye contact, and comforting and playful physical contact.

3     *"Apparently" sensitive.* The adult is sensitive in some ways, but the observer finds it difficult to give this relationship a "clean bill of health." Adult inconsistency in behavior may be one telltale sign (including the signs of inconsistency discussed above).

1     *Highly insensitive.* This adult displays few areas of strength in interaction with the child.

## Adult Structuring

5     *Optimal structuring.* The adult lets the child lead while providing a supportive framework; that is, the adult offers the child the chance to explore and do things while providing a framework on which the child can build.

.

.

.

1     *Nonoptimal structuring.* The adult sets no limits and provides no structure for the child.

## Adult Nonintrusiveness

5    *Nonintrusive.* The interaction is nonintrusive, smooth, and "spacious."

.

.

.

1    *Intrusive.* The adult controls the interaction, sometimes even physically, punishing or manhandling, and jumps in to do too much for the child, showing a lack of respect and space for not only the child's wishes but also abilities.

## Adult Nonhostility

5    *Nonhostile.* There are no expressions of overt or covert hostility toward the child that can be discerned by the observer. The general emotional climate appears nonhostile.

.

.

.

1    *Markedly and overtly hostile.* This adult is overtly harsh, abrasive, and demeaning—facially and/or vocally. Adult behavior is threatening and/or frightening.

## Child Responsiveness to the Adult

5    *Optimal in responsiveness.* He or she generally shows pleasure and eagerness in responding to the adult's comments, suggestions, questions, and demonstrations.

.

.

.

1    *Clearly nonoptimal in responsiveness.* The child rarely shows emotional and behavioral responsiveness (of the optimal kind) when engaged with the adult and rarely responds to an adult initiative. Alternatively, the child may be overly responsive to the adult.

## Child Involvement with the Adult

5         *Optimal in involving behaviors.* The child seems interested in engaging the adult in interaction without compromising autonomous pursuits.

.

.

.

1         *Clearly nonoptimal in involving behaviors..* This child does not optimally orient toward the adult. This child does not show a good balance between involving behaviors and autonomous pursuits at all. The child may be over-involving of the adult.

## Section 1
## Emotional Availability Report[2]
## (for use by parents with children younger than two years of age)

| | Almost Never 1 | Sometimes 2 | 3 | 4 | Almost Always 5 |
|---|---|---|---|---|---|
| 1. My baby is upset whenever I leave the room and seems to play mostly near me. | ☐ | ☐ | ☐ | ☐ | ☐ |
| 2. My baby doesn't seem to notice when I come back into the room. | ☐ | ☐ | ☐ | ☐ | ☐ |
| 3. My baby doesn't crawl/walk to me much. | ☐ | ☐ | ☐ | ☐ | ☐ |
| 4. I wish my baby were happier when with me. | ☐ | ☐ | ☐ | ☐ | ☐ |
| 5. My baby looks at me and listens to me when I try to talk to him (or her). | ☐ | ☐ | ☐ | ☐ | ☐ |
| 6. My baby likes to be with me the most. | ☐ | ☐ | ☐ | ☐ | ☐ |
| 7. My baby is lots of fun to be around. | ☐ | ☐ | ☐ | ☐ | ☐ |
| 8. My baby is very independent and mostly likes to play on his (or her) own. | ☐ | ☐ | ☐ | ☐ | ☐ |
| 9. My baby seems to "light up" when he (or she) sees me. | ☐ | ☐ | ☐ | ☐ | ☐ |
| 10. After I leave the room, my baby seems really happy that I've come back. | ☐ | ☐ | ☐ | ☐ | ☐ |
| 11. My baby barely notices me. | ☐ | ☐ | ☐ | ☐ | ☐ |
| 12. My baby is "cranky" most of the time. | ☐ | ☐ | ☐ | ☐ | ☐ |
| 13. My baby seems to understand what I mean most of the time. | ☐ | ☐ | ☐ | ☐ | ☐ |
| 14. I feel my baby tries to communicate with me. | ☐ | ☐ | ☐ | ☐ | ☐ |
| 15. When I try to play with my baby, he (or she) seems to be busy and mostly moves away. | ☐ | ☐ | ☐ | ☐ | ☐ |
| 16. It's hard to get my baby to play with me for very long. | ☐ | ☐ | ☐ | ☐ | ☐ |
| 17. I wish my baby could play a little more on his (or her) own. | ☐ | ☐ | ☐ | ☐ | ☐ |

| | Almost Never 1 | 2 | Sometimes 3 | 4 | Almost Always 5 |
|---|---|---|---|---|---|
| 18. My baby and I have lots of fun together. | ☐ | ☐ | ☐ | ☐ | ☐ |
| 19. When my baby seems to not want to play with me, I feel hurt. | ☐ | ☐ | ☐ | ☐ | ☐ |
| 20. I don't feel close to this baby. | ☐ | ☐ | ☐ | ☐ | ☐ |
| 21. I try to see things from my baby's perspective. | ☐ | ☐ | ☐ | ☐ | ☐ |
| 22. When things go wrong, I get bent out of shape easily. | ☐ | ☐ | ☐ | ☐ | ☐ |
| 23. I am usually in a good mood around my baby. | ☐ | ☐ | ☐ | ☐ | ☐ |
| 24. When things go wrong, I tend to be flexible. | ☐ | ☐ | ☐ | ☐ | ☐ |
| 25. Even if my baby doesn't get it right, I let him (or her) have the experience. | ☐ | ☐ | ☐ | ☐ | ☐ |
| 26. It's difficult for me to say "goodbye" or separate from my child when I leave the house or leave him (or her) with a sitter. | ☐ | ☐ | ☐ | ☐ | ☐ |
| 27. I shadow my child's every step as if it could be his (or her) last, and I worry much too much. | ☐ | ☐ | ☐ | ☐ | ☐ |
| 28. It is hard to soothe my baby and he (or she) seems to be distressed a lot. | ☐ | ☐ | ☐ | ☐ | ☐ |

## Scoring Your Test:

Questions #5, #6, #7, #9, #10, #13, #14, #18, #21, #23, #24, and #25: If you answered 3, 4, or 5 on these questions, your EA is relatively high. Although individuals can have some low responses on these questions, if you received a total score greater than 36, you are engaging in a relatively good level of emotional availability.

Questions #1, #2, #3, #4, #8, #11, #12, #15, #16, #17, #19, #20, #22, #26, #27, and #28: If you answered 1 or 2 for these questions, your EA with your child is pretty good. If you scored a total of 16-32 points on these questions, again, you are in a relatively good level of emotional availability.

## Section 2
## Emotional Availability Report[3]
## (for use by parents with children older than two years of age)

| | Almost Never | Sometimes | | | Almost Always |
|---|---|---|---|---|---|
| | 1 | 2 | 3 | 4 | 5 |
| 1. My child is upset a lot. | ☐ | ☐ | ☐ | ☐ | ☐ |
| 2. My child doesn't talk to me much about what goes on at preschool/school. | ☐ | ☐ | ☐ | ☐ | ☐ |
| 3. I wish my child smiled more and seemed happier. | ☐ | ☐ | ☐ | ☐ | ☐ |
| 4. My child listens to me when I talk to him (or her). | ☐ | ☐ | ☐ | ☐ | ☐ |
| 5. My child seems happy when with other children. | ☐ | ☐ | ☐ | ☐ | ☐ |
| 6. My child has lots of fun with me. | ☐ | ☐ | ☐ | ☐ | ☐ |
| 7. My child has few friends. | ☐ | ☐ | ☐ | ☐ | ☐ |
| 8. My child seems sad to me. | ☐ | ☐ | ☐ | ☐ | ☐ |
| 9. Others (e.g., teachers, my friends) have commented on my child not seeming happy. | ☐ | ☐ | ☐ | ☐ | ☐ |
| 10. My child and I do a lot together. | ☐ | ☐ | ☐ | ☐ | ☐ |
| 11. My child listens to me when I discipline him (or her). | ☐ | ☐ | ☐ | ☐ | ☐ |
| 12. My child tries to talk to me when he (or she) has something on his (or her) mind. | ☐ | ☐ | ☐ | ☐ | ☐ |
| 13. When I try to talk to my child, he (or she) seems disinterested in my joining in. | ☐ | ☐ | ☐ | ☐ | ☐ |
| 14. My child likes to be on his (or her) own and is a bit of a loner. | ☐ | ☐ | ☐ | ☐ | ☐ |
| 15. I feel I don't have a lot of control and my child is the one with control around here. | ☐ | ☐ | ☐ | ☐ | ☐ |
| 16. I don't feel like I know this child. | ☐ | ☐ | ☐ | ☐ | ☐ |
| 17. When my child seems not to want to play with me, I feel hurt. | ☐ | ☐ | ☐ | ☐ | ☐ |

|  | Almost Never 1 | 2 | Sometimes 3 | 4 | Almost Always 5 |
|---|---|---|---|---|---|
| 18. My child cries a lot and seems to get bent out of shape easily. | ☐ | ☐ | ☐ | ☐ | ☐ |
| 19. I listen to my child when he (or she) tries to explain things to me. | ☐ | ☐ | ☐ | ☐ | ☐ |
| 20. I try to see things from my child's perspective. | ☐ | ☐ | ☐ | ☐ | ☐ |
| 21. When things go wrong, I get bent out of shape easily. | ☐ | ☐ | ☐ | ☐ | ☐ |
| 22. I am usually in a good mood around my child. | ☐ | ☐ | ☐ | ☐ | ☐ |
| 23. When things go wrong, I tend to be flexible. | ☐ | ☐ | ☐ | ☐ | ☐ |
| 24. When I see that my child isn't getting it right, I jump in to correct him (or her). | ☐ | ☐ | ☐ | ☐ | ☐ |
| 25. It's difficult for me to separate from my child for school, sleepovers, playdates. | ☐ | ☐ | ☐ | ☐ | ☐ |
| 26. I shadow my child's every step as if it could be his (or her) last, and I worry. | ☐ | ☐ | ☐ | ☐ | ☐ |
| 27. My child seems to need a lot of assurances and reassurances of my caring and attention and seems to use distress to get attention. | ☐ | ☐ | ☐ | ☐ | ☐ |

## Scoring Your Test:

Questions #4, #5, #6, #10, #11, #12, #19, #20, #22, #23: If you answered 3, 4, or 5 on these questions, your EA is relatively high. Although individuals can have some low responses on these questions, if you received a total score greater than 35, you may be engaging in a relatively good level of emotional availability.

Questions #1, #2, #3, #7, #8, #9, #13, #14, #15, #16, #17, #18, #21, #24, #25, #26, and #27: If you answered 1 or 2 for these questions, your EA with your child is good. If you scored a total of 17-34 points on these questions, again, you are in a relatively good level of emotional availability.

# 4 Being Aware of Emotional Availability/ Unavailability in all Your Relationships

Emotional availability in the parent-child relationship is important because it can help a child feel an enduring sense of security in the parent-child attachment and consequently make a child feel more secure in this insecure world. Some individuals will easily connect to these ideas and see that these skills translate to the wider world. Others may be more skeptical.

One businessman client I had been seeing in my private practice told me that he did not see the value of spending so much time becoming "emotionally available, as you say." But he decided to try the ideas anyway. He later described to me that not only was he a better father and husband (the qualities he had been seeking to improve), but he was also better at his job as a CEO of a highly recognized corporation. He found that his skills of emotional availability have helped him in the workplace. Being more sensitive toward employees, structuring of their efforts, nonintrusive in his suggestions and actions but available and connected, and nonhostile and better emotionally regulated when interacting with them has helped him keep a great team of players at work. He has built quite a reputation as a nice boss!

Another client, a 60-year-old female, and her husband are now raising her three grandchildren. Her son married a woman overseas while stationed in Europe, and they had three children in five years. With too many cultural and religious issues separating them, the young couple eventually divorced, but not before the biological mother was addicted to street drugs and began to seriously neglect the children. The grandmother stepped in and is now raising the children, lest they be taken into foster care, and she needs the skills of emotional availability. She recalls having "missed that" when she was raising her two boys in the context of an early bad marriage, and she is now seeing her grandparenting as a "second chance" at using these skills. These skills can be learned, and re-learned, with practice! Although she is a very busy and successful businesswoman, she is grateful that she has a stable family life and financial circumstances that enable her to become truly emotionally available to her grandchildren—in a way she was not able to do when she was raising her first family. This is a very hopeful message.

How can we apply the same principles of emotional availability to other relationships, such as peer-peer relationships or couples' relationships? Essentially, the same system is used, with the exception that for equal partners, all six dimensions are used *for each of the equal partners*. Parent-child (and in particular parent-infant) interactions are called "dances" due to the beautiful give and take that goes on in these interactions, but I have not used that term in the previous chapters, mainly because I wanted to underscore the term "relationship." Children need to experience the important adults in their lives as real, genuine, and long-lasting relationship figures. With respect to equal partners, I use the term "dance" in this chapter merely to illustrate that there isn't necessarily the same level of commitment and the assumption of being older and wiser, but there is nonetheless communication using the principles of love, developed through the science of emotional availability.

Before we get to the test, you should begin to think about each of the six questions. Think about a peer-peer relationship for children at any age (including potentially the relationship between two teenagers); an adult-adult relationship for people who are unrelated to each other but who have an ongoing connection (such as co-workers); an adult-adult relationship of related people, in which one is the parent and the other is the adult child; as well as a romantic relationship between two adults, whether heterosexual or homosexual. As you consider each question and think of where you might rate this specific relationship between two people, know that you can use this system in the context of only one relationship at a time.

## 1a. How Sensitive Are You with This Dance Partner?

## 1b. Is Your Dance Partner Sensitive toward You?

Sensitivity is the ability to read another and be emotionally and openly communicative with that person. Sensitivity is the tool that allows an individual to create a strong emotional connection. It refers to a variety of qualities in the individual—in particular, affective range (usually tipped toward the positive), reading of the other's communications, interest in and ability to resolve conflicts smoothly, and so on. As you can see, sensitivity in peer-peer relationships would be based on a child or a teen being able to read the cues of the other individual and to respond appropriately. This sounds like "common sense" and common emotional communication, but given no set of rules and regulations on interactions and the extent of both physical and relational bullying in schools, it seems an important primer with which to train the next generation. Although it is common sense that people can and should read each other's cues and communications and respond appropriately and also interact in generally (and genuinely!) positive ways, why do we have so many emotionally unavailable relationships going on all around us! Consider the vignettes below, one describing the relational dances of young children and the other of teenagers.

> At child care, Rosella seemed by nature to be a "loner" and rarely talked or played with the other children. As a group of children were building towers and knocking them down, with hearty laughter, she looked on in a longing way. The other children barely noticed her, and, in fact, Leonardo almost walked into her in his excitement. As she continued in child care and the professionals began to talk and play with her in fun ways, Rosella, too, became used to emotionally available relationships at the center. One day, she and Michela were seen holding hands and giggling together on the playground. Rosella no longer had a loner temperament.

> Anne, a 16-year-old teenager, is interacting with Sandy, her 16-year-old "buddy," in the cafeteria. Sandy and Anne talk for a few seconds, and then Sandy turns her back on Anne

abruptly, signaling emotional unavailability. Anne continues to initiate interactions with Sandy, but soon looks forlorn and rejected (sensitivity dimension). She continues to stand there. The next day, Anne quickly approaches Sandy at the lockers and nervously but excitedly tells her of a great day at soccer (sensitivity dimension). Sandy shrugs and moves away. This saga continues each day, with Anne feeling further and further dejected, but also continuing the same unwelcome initiations toward Sandy. Although Sandy may be the individual rejecting and emotionally unavailable in this relationship, Anne is insensitive in that she is either not reading Sandy's communications or she is misreading them. Further, she loses much of her positivity.

As you think about evaluating your own sensitivity and evaluating that of others with whom you have relationships, consider the components of sensitivity taken specifically from Chapter 2.

- Predominantly positive, in terms of both facial and vocal expressiveness.

- Appropriately responsive to the circumstances and the other's emotions.

- Displaying congruence between verbal and nonverbal expression.

- Accurately perceptive and appropriately responsive.

- Aware of timing.

- Flexible in terms of attention, behavior, and approach.

- Showing acceptance of the other.

- Empathic.

- Able to handle conflict.

Rather than taking these components of sensitivity one by one, as was done in Chapter 2, let's look at them as a whole package. When thinking about relationships that go right, all of the dimensions seem so obvious. But, what about relationships that we hear about in the news and other dysfunctional relationships people experience? Which of these qualities seem to elude the radar?

In truly dysfunctional relationships related to abuse (physical or verbal), perpetrators often are able to show the positive qualities outlined above. Those who know the perpetrators depict individuals who were really nice and positive.

> In terms of the language of love, it is crucial (in both adult-child relationships, in peer-peer relationships, and in adult-adult relationships) to attend to an aspect of sensitivity that is little talked about and little understood, but that is part of the scoring system of emotional availability.

That aspect is "inconsistent sensitivity" or "apparent sensitivity." As you may note from studying the system, individuals can seem sensitive without really being so. The congruence of verbal and nonverbal channels, empathy, and, most immediately, affect (that very first item on the list—the countenance on the face, the lifetime of facial expressions etched on the face, not just smiling or trying to seem pleasing) are important, telling, and discriminating between the *apparently* positive or sensitive and the *really* sensitive. Although I am a clinical psychologist, I wish not to go into diagnostic categories here, but to make the system applicable to all interactions. I see that individuals in daily life show significant variability in this quality, and it is up to the interactive partner to discern what is high in sensitivity and what is apparently sensitive, which is in the mid-range of the scale. For this, note that we need to attend to affect, empathy, and the congruence between different channels of communication, including verbal and nonverbal (tone of voice and body language). Even though some may think of the psychopathic personality here, I would like to take this opportunity to say that people who are normal but who care less about a particular relationship, or those who wish to keep it going or need to keep it going without commitment of emotional resources, also show this quality. In other words, I am not describing something that is a quality of the *individual* necessarily, but a quality of the *relationship*, and as long as the interactive partner does not read these cues, the interactive partner, too, is less sensitive!

> Eva was always eager to help others and was consistently in a positive, upbeat mood, as far as anyone could see. She and her live-in boyfriend, Hans, were reputable, local business owners at the outdoor mall downtown. Although they were relatively

new to town, people saw them as friendly and ready to help when anyone needed them. They seemed like perfect friends, perfect neighbors, and perfect tenants. It was quite a surprise, then, when the police sought them out for methamphetamine possession, and numerous drug paraphernalia were found in their vacated house, along with numerous professional-quality appliances to extract juice from fruits and vegetables—juicers. On a tip, they had skipped town and left everything behind, along with their cover for illegal drug possession and (likely) sales. As well, they left behind medical records indicating that Eva had made a number of recent emergency room visits. Police questioning regarding these perfectly fine neighbors indicated that yelling and, potentially, screaming in terror could be heard at times.

> Intimate partner violence occurs within the privacy of the home, and sometimes only telltale signs are left behind. Many of the people who are engaged in such severely dysfunctional relationships are the very people others view as lovely people. Thus, it is important to think about "apparent sensitivity" (all that glitters is not gold), and to have that perspective as an aspect of the present rather than as 20-20 hindsight.

Individuals' affect (pseudo positive rather than authentically positive and genuine) and body language need to be attended to more carefully, which can be done if one makes a point of doing so! This is the power of understanding the universal language of love—it is not a surprise if you are looking for the possibility of apparent sensitivity out in the real world of relationships! Apparent sensitivity is not always associated with drug use or possession or abusive relationships. It can also be there in approximately 10 percent of normal relationships—meaning that people are simply not as sensitive as they may appear and that they are likely not to engage in healthy relationships.

The vignettes in this chapter introduced Rosella, who was initially a loner and did not seem to be able to join in the fun and games of the other children, followed by Anne, who similarly did not "read" the cues and communications of her dancing partner. Both would be seen as low in terms of these specific dances during their specific episodes. In contrast, Eva and Hans appeared sensitive, but were really not so, as they danced with each other and with other partners. In fact, their life was built upon a tenuous reality based on the *appearance* of being nice and good—but their positive affect was not genuine. They would be scored in the mid-range of the sensitivity test shown toward the end of this chapter because there is an inconsistency about them that could be seen and that was palpable, as for example, Hans's nice and pleasing voice combined with eyes that seemed violent, and Eva's accommodating behaviors combined with facial affect that was "put on" for the occasion. They knew how to present themselves as sensitive, but the "inconsistencies" in their nonverbal channels of communication and between their words and their actions created falseness.

The optimally sensitive individual does not have to—but may—have false starts, mis-steps, and corrections, and is not necessarily as polished as Eva and Hans's dance with others. In fact, normal interactions are full of needed repairs. Genuine affect is the key and the most important criterion in the decision matrix to go on the sensitivity scale. It is not about being overly emotional or overly positive or overly fake, but it is about genuine affect, with some range from positive to negative. Consider the three scenarios below, illustrating optimal sensitivity.

> Consalata had entered kindergarten within the last month and was generally a quiet observer. One day, she saw a group of children holding hands and playing ring-around-the-rosy on the playground at recess, and she stood nearby, smiling and seemingly engaged as a spectator. She then slowly began to move closer to them and moved into the circle, laughing and giggling like all of them.

> Fourteen-year-old José loved ballet, but he was the only male in the class at his level, now that his best ballet buddy moved to a different town. He felt awkward at first, but then started chatting with some of the girls, who often went out to lunch together during weekend rehearsals for Peter Pan—without inviting him. That did not feel good, and he stayed behind at the studio to do his homework. He often thought about going to a different ballet school. But he continued to talk to the girls and enjoyed their company during class. One day, the girls said,

"Hey, wanna come with us, we're going to Starbucks to study." Not sure if he looked nonchalant or beaming, and thinking he showed some of both, he walked over to Starbucks with them, and from that point on, he was part of "the group."

Audrey was a healthy 86 years old, and the mother of an adult son and daughter who had their own families. Although she lived with her daughter in Korea, far away from her native England and far from those who spoke English (and often felt rattled due to a lack of any friends in Korea), she was always careful and supportive with her words and deeds. Even when she lost her husband some 30 years ago, she was as concerned about understanding her children's bereavement of their father as her own sense of loss, and often forgot about her own problems, including financial issues.

## 2a. Do You Structure and Guide the Dance?

## 2b. Is Your Dance Partner Structuring with You?

Outside of caregiver-child relationships, the meaning of structuring continues! In fact, all of the EA dimensions are life-span ideas and can be applicable in understanding relationships at any age. Structuring is about support in an unforced way.

- Support in the context of exploration and pursuits

- Support in the context of conversation

- Having clear limits and boundaries for the relationship

- Freedom to provide well-appointed suggestions

- Verbal support as well as nonverbal

- Support that is welcomed

- Support, but not too much!

Individuals support each other and even "save each other" from themselves. When one partner has a "weakness," the other often steps in and plays to his or her strengths. Interactive partners (who are appropriately structuring) also support each other in their individual activities and show interest in those activities. When one makes a gaffe, the other might build up the conversation again rather than honing in and blowing it out of proportion. But the language of love does not support unending support, especially if it is not welcome (there is a dyadic or relational quality to all of this!). Also, too much support that is either not welcomed or that is overwhelming is like too much of a good thing.

Teenagers support each other as they are going through school and help each other with homework. They also help each other with social problems. There may be some conflicts and struggles, but their learning of the universal language of love continues in a good trajectory if they are generally supporting each other with new pursuits or helping each other during conversations or exchanges. There is, however, a limit to how much they can assume this aspect of the role. A general level of interest in the others' activities and support is a good thing, and the recognition of when someone is not being structuring is also a necessity.

> Nicolletta and her friends in high school are in a very rigorous curriculum. Many of the girls in the group stay after school and study together, test each other, call each other on the telephone when they have questions, and "cry on each others' shoulders" when the things get rough. But the occasional bullying does occur, such as when Ester says, "I don't think her science fair project was as good as she thought."

In adult-adult relationships, structuring is more clearly seen, as is the case for parent-child relationships. Only one person doing the lion's share of structuring and the other basking in it does not seem like a good translation of the universal language of love, and in a solid relationship mere awareness of it can turn it around so that structuring is used by both members of the communication. Again, structuring occurs in the context of a relationship and is not a quality or trait of an individual.

> Paola had been a carefree bachelor well into his 40s, but now he was not only adoring of his wife, Jodie, and an involved father, he was also supportive and helped Jodie reach heights in her career that she had not imagined could be possible. She received her MBA, opened up her own mortgage company, and also did home reconstruction. Paola, who was by training a civil engineer, actually obtained his independent realtor's

license to help sell Jodie's homes. As his second job, he showed her homes and took many of the calls. He made suggestions and participated in her career. The support and structuring were very helpful to Jodie's multimillion-dollar business, and to their business collaboration and close family life.

However, structuring attempts are not always welcomed by the other, and then one needs to decide whether the lack of welcoming involves a safety issue, and hence is worth the resistance. Where there is some clash, usually the current relationship tests in the mid-range, suggesting that the dance needs to be practiced some more so that both partners in the dance feel that the tempo is just right.

Audrey's daughter, Josephine, has liked to structure her mother's activities, since Audrey fell down as she was going to the bathroom in the middle of the night (but did not have a fracture) about 10 months ago. Josephine says that her mother needs to take her cell phone on her outings and needs to call her at certain points. Further, Josephine has expressed that she prefers that her mother not go anywhere without her. Occasionally, Audrey "disobeys" and goes out and uses the bus system, and she comes back with a bag full of groceries to contribute to the household.

Obviously, Audrey prefers to have her freedom to come and go as she pleases, without having to report to Josephine; yet, Josephine is over-structuring. The relationship may need renegotiation so that both feel comfortable with the level of structuring and guidance needed for a healthy 86-year-old!

In contrast to Josephine, take note of the following scenario, illustrating an extreme of unstructuring behavior:

Josephine's friend, Anne, also originally from the United Kingdom, rarely wanted to see her 80-year-old mother, Shannon. In fact, she had a rule—when Shannon came to visit her in Korea, she was allowed to stay for no more than one month. Anne believed that Shannon's lengthy visits had been disruptive to her marriage, which had recently ended. Shannon was still a good driver and enjoyed going places on her own. Shannon would come and go as she pleased, and Anne rarely asked where she had been!

# 3a. Are You Available in This Relationship without Being Intrusive?

# 3b. Is Your Dance Partner Available to You without Being Intrusive?

Intrusive behavior can take many forms. If adults set the pace and tone of interactions too often, this can be intrusive. Asking too many questions or directing the course of interaction rather than letting the other individual often take the lead are signs of intrusive behavior. Even initiating too much or too frequently, without being invited or welcomed in some way, or when the other individual is preoccupied with other tasks, can be seen as intrusiveness. Often, mere awareness of the universal language of love is enough to bring things back to a more balanced level.

More difficult situations are the following:

- An overdeveloped need to control the environment

- Viewing your role in a relationship as the sole leader

- Subtle or not-so-subtle personality dysfunctions—an adult with narcissistic tendencies (read "self-centered") might feel a sense of entitlement

- Issues about control in the family who raised us

- Achievement, overachievement, or perfectionistic needs

- Being too available

- Caring too much!

Optimal nonintrusiveness is an important aspect of the universal language of love, and it is in this way that the individual gives space to the other—space to "return the serve." It is important to remember that intrusiveness is determined not solely by one adult's actions, but also by the interactive partner's emotional response. If an interactive partner cannot give space and needs to control and lead, this is a problem, at least potentially, in the short or long run. Many such people can feel a sense of narcissism, which gives them the entitlement to control conversation and to control decisions that are made. Often, but not always, the reasons can be benign, such as caring too much for the other individual. But intrusiveness can lead to "chasing" the other and does not give the other individual the gratifying and satisfying part of the equation that involves returning the serve.

This is important not only in caregiver-child relationships from the very beginning, but also in adult-adult relationships. It never ceases to be important! Individuals of all ages need space to grow and feel good, and crowding that space, even for the most lofty of reasons—such as sisterly love, brotherly love, romantic love, and so on—can make the other feel not trusted with that space. The extent of space is negotiated by the interactive partners. Further, being too available is also a relationship quality. Spending every minute together is totally nonintrusive when both are signing on for this, but one initiating this process on a regular basis when not being welcomed or sought out by the other is too much emotional availability, and again, associated with the use of space. Space—giving it, being able to ask for it, and respecting the need for it—are important in the dance of relationships, particularly relationships that can last the test of time, such as caregiver-child relationships, long-term committed relationships, best friendships, and so on.

In the last story, Paola was supportive of Jodie, but not intrusive. He would defer to Jodie on decisions related to the sale of her properties, and he did not take over. He was available and helpful without smothering. In contrast, consider the next story.

> Brian was insecure about his relationship with Perry, especially as Perry was getting close to receiving his nursing degree. Brian wondered whether he would be interesting enough for Perry as time went on. Brian became over-controlling, asking exactly where Perry had been and with which friends, asking why it had taken him so long to get home, and basically making Perry miserable with his worries, which felt immature and smothering to Perry.

Some of the qualities that are included in the view of nonintrusiveness are:

- Following the other's lead and not going beyond what the other "feels" is intrusive

- Not interrupting verbally

- Not constantly commanding, directing

- Not physically interfering or manhandling or other physical gestures that are unwelcomed

Going to a younger age level, where the skills of emotional availability—the language of love—is in the formative stage, parents and other adults can be especially helpful to their children as they navigate these waters. As a result of these experiences, some children may move toward their teen years feeling immensely confident about this language, whereas others may move into the teen years feeling less and less confident about these skills based on how they have been deciphering these emotional communications during their lives. Consider Cory, in the next vignette, who wanted so very much to be invited to social events.

> Cory, 10 years old, did cold calling to classmates to see if they would like to come over and play with him. He was lonely and his mother told him that by taking the initiative, he would make friends. Cory picked up the phone, and in an overeager tone, said, "Hi, it's Cory. Would you like to come over to my house?" to Tamaya, to whom he had talked only one time in the cafeteria, to ask for the correct time. When Tamaya did not remember who he was, Cory then called Nicky, who said he was busy. Because Nicky showed minimal signs of interest, Cory called Nicky again the following weekend, to ask again. Needless to say, Cory was "chasing" without having a connection, and this seemed intrusive to others. The dance was such that the pursuit or intrusive moving toward others made them move back one step. Had Cory taken a step back in the dance to give others a chance to move toward him, it could have been different. Yet Cory continued this trend because he was unaware of the language of love, and he grew to be a 14-year-old who perceived the world as a pretty unfriendly place. In contrast to how he had been at 10 years of age—eager to make friends—at 14 years of age, Cory was quiet and retiring and rarely made overtures toward others. His spirit was broken!

In the mid-range of nonintrusiveness are "benign" forms of behavior—benign because the intentions are good, but one individual is smothering the other, and so the effect can be negative. See the example below.

> Arthur recently met Ali at an art history class in college, but since they met, they've been spending a lot more time together. Although they seem both to be pleased about meeting each other frequently—to discuss their assignments for the class, for

coffee, and for meals—Arthur seems already to be overprotective, asking whether Ali has been driving carefully, dressing warmly, and so forth, and sometimes it seems to Ali like too much unwelcomed care and attention. Arthur is able to "read" Ali's reactions and begins to give her more space, which then increases the closeness between the two friends.

## 4a. Is There Any Overt or Covert Hostility Present?

## 4b. Is Your Dance Partner Showing Overt or Covert Hostility?

Hostility in the home environment was broached in the earlier chapter about the caregiver-child relationship and cannot be overemphasized in the context of adult-adult relationships in which there are children in the home. There is no such thing as hostility of one member toward the other member of a relationship and keeping it surgically encapsulated when children are within earshot or eyeshot.

Some conflict, and particularly its successful resolution, is thought to be a positive attribute for children. What this means is that children might get to see their parents argue and then figure out a resolution to the conflict. Homes that are fully nonconflictual may never show children that ups and downs are sometimes inevitable parts of day-to-day living. If parents shield children from normal vicissitudes, it is thought that these children may not learn these conflict-resolution skills.

But beyond a very moderate amount that remains generally peaceful, hostility and conflict are not good for children. Hence, hostility (covert or overt) in the couple's relationship is an important background quality of the home, and whether or not hostility is directed toward the child, this background quality inherent in the couple's relationship is key to setting the emotional temperature of the home.

In adult-adult relationships, the most concerning aspects of hostility are, of course, perpetration of violence, including intimate partner violence—the majority of which is directed toward women—and abuse against children. Violence is the endpoint of expressions of hostility. Once one act of intimate partner violence or child abuse is committed, these are difficult relational dynamics to stop. Usually, such violence is predicted by earlier bouts of violence, in one form or another, but often the "victim" does not know about the earlier history. What are the telltale signs to look for in an interactive partner or potential mate?

> Hillary was a full-of-life freshman at a well-respected state university. She was doing really well in her classes and making many new friends in her dormitory. Her only self-perceived problem was her weight, which tended to fluctuate. She always viewed herself as obese, although others could see her attractiveness. Partly because of her preoccupation with her weight, she was surprised when the sophomore she had a crush on and secretly called "the hunk" was also interested in her. She was very outgoing and easy to know. He was taciturn but happy in the relationship. The relationship lasted more than two years, and, again to her surprise, it was Hillary who realized that she wanted out of the relationship, mainly because she realized that "the hunk" was inward to a point that scared her, and their differences loomed large. Although her friendliness helped her get into the relationship, it was difficult to figure out how she would get out of it because "the hunk" clearly did not want to let go. When she finally did break up with him, he beat her miserably. She remembered that he had mentioned some physical conflict in a previous relationship as well, but she realized she had been blind to it. She said that she should have and could have seen this coming by how he lost his temper during the relationship and would glare through her.

---

**Past behavior is the best indicator of future behavior! A history of lack of empathy toward life (be it a child, adult, or animal, or in thoughts or threats about living things) is not a good sign.**

---

How else can you tell? The nonhostility component of emotional availability can be a guide (see the test at the end of this chapter), and one should look for "leaks" of hostility in the form of irritations, frustrations, teasing, and the like, as well as negative emotions that the individual is finding difficult to regulate. The more the stressor, the more difficult the negative emotion regulation, but signs that a person is having difficulty with anger management, be it in the extreme (e.g., yelling or throwing things) or on the lower end (e.g., joking with a tinge of hostility, seemingly unaware of physical boundaries) are important early signs. Not all cases of violence can be predicted from a past history of violence or from the early signs of anger management problems, but a look at our relationship partners in this way can be an important exercise in awareness, as women and children are most affected. It is surprising that so many women stay in relationships with an established history of hostility, even staying until their lives end. Seeking professional help to guide in the process is essential. Early awareness of interpersonal hostility *before* the relationship is an intimate one is far better!

What about peer-peer relationships? Certainly, obvious hostility, such as physical fighting, is clear. But, what about relational aggression?

> Louise was very interpersonally skilled and a "popular" girl at her middle school. She often started or ended her sentences with "honey," such as "Do you want me to bake you a cake, honey?" Because she was so nice and helpful as a friend, it was difficult for the girls in the group to see that she was covertly hostile, and on a regular basis. "Kathy's clothes are slutty," she would say to Therese. "Why is Margie mad at me?" she would say to Kathy. And so on.
>
> It was important for the members of this clique to know about Louise, who created a covertly hostile climate within the group. The girls generally saw her as sweet—until they began to share these statements with each other—and then they began to respond to some of the covertly hostile comments in a more positive, resilient way, such as "I'm sure Margie is not mad—she's just serious because she has a test today."

Supporting our children to gain skills to become resilient in the face of others' verbally or physically aggressive behaviors is important. Schools address physical bullying, but they rarely address more invisible signs of hostility, such as exclusions, rejections, and gossip. Through relating to our children by using the language of love (see Chapter 2), adults set the stage for children's learning of this language. Any derailing of this track can be corrected if one remembers this language and how it can be used effectively.

> Sam was a dedicated spouse and father, but with a covertly (and sometimes, overtly) hostile streak. Although he never showed full-blown road rage, a trip to the market always involved an expletive or two as he drove there. Once at the

market, he was usually frustrated with the long line and "rolled his eyes" at the man with a shopping cart that was chockful of groceries and canned foods to last him a month. Once back in the car with his family, he would ask if his son Andy had done his chores (cleaned his room and bathroom, played cello for one hour, played the clarinet for three hours), and when Andy said that he had not, Sam would launch his usual diatribe about how he was no longer going to pay $45 to the cello classes and $80 for the clarinet classes, and would threaten that the classes would be history. He would yell all the way home. When his son talked back, he would say, "Okay, soon enough you'll be rid of me." Once home, he would begin to calm down (particularly because his wife would state that it was wrong to be so aggressive) and then apologize to his son. For both the wife and son, the stress hormones running through their bodies were almost palpable, and yet Sam had no clue that he had emotion-regulation problems. Ho also did not realize he used threats to control or make a point.

In contrast to the above, example, consider this next story.

Larry was a very calm, upbeat, optimistic person, and although money was tight because his wife had recently lost her job, Larry seemed to remain solid and nonhostile. When out driving with his son, Doug, he worried a little about his son's purple hair. Out loud, he said, "Your hair is purple, Doug. You know, I also had my ways of trying to stand out from the crowd when I was your age—if that's the worst thing you can do to be "different," son, you're a pretty great kid!"

## 5a. Are You Emotionally Responsive to This Dance Partner?

## 5b. Is This Dance Partner Emotionally Responsive to You?

Just like in the caregiver-child relationship, the only way to tell if a relationship is working well is to look at the other individual. The emotional quality of the other's responses is the key. If the other ignores or generally appears bland or blasé, the relationship is not working! In peer-peer relationships, this is called peer rejection or peer neglect, and in adult-adult relationships, it can be called the same. If the other is not enthusiastic and engaged, generally speaking, then the relationship is not an emotionally available one. All too often, people invest more and more into relationships that are not working in the sense of the language of love.

What is important is not just the response itself, but the emotional quality of the response from the other individual. Conversely, we have seen situations in which the significant adult doesn't reach out to the other or initiate much contact, and the relationship partner nonetheless continues and further invests in the relationship. Another aspect of the interactive partner's behavior that indicates lack of optimal responsiveness is what we call a "negative cycle of connectedness." The other may be negative or otherwise "act out" in myriad ways as part of being in a relationship. Not only is such behavior not optimal responsiveness—it is negative responsiveness. Very often, in adult-adult relationships, the very individuals who are seen as a "loving husband" or the "perfect wife" are individuals who have been "acting up" or "acting out" in the relationship when others are not there to see.

Thus, the stage presence may be different than the usual presence in the relationship. Insecure emotional bonds can further grow, mainly because one member of the relationship is not emotionally responsive. This is the obvious part.

> **The less obvious part in the form of human communication is that the other individual is not "reading" these cues and continues to invest in an emotionally unavailable relationship.**

It is important here to reiterate what I wrote in relation to caregiver-child relationships as a basis for the language of love in other relationships.

> Children who are optimally emotionally responsive to a specific significant other [adult] usually demonstrate a happy and content countenance. They are content pursuing autonomous activities but they also respond in a positive way toward that adult at appropriate points. Their response generally shows pleasure and eagerness without any sense of urgency or necessity. They smile or laugh appropriately, and usually attend to

adults' comments, questions, suggestions, and demonstrations with ease. Emotionally responsive children may not respond to every request, however, especially when they are engrossed in play. But there is the sense that, for the most part, the child is comfortable with and willing to respond to the overtures in this adult-child relationship.

If the emotional responsiveness is not at the highest level, the child may respond but seem unenthusiastic about doing so. The child may respond slowly and reluctantly, continuing play as if he or she didn't hear the adult. The child who always responds to the adult in an overeager, overly bright way is also not optimal . . . this may indicate a reversal in roles (the child feeling like he or she has to take care of the adult, rather than the other way around). In the most serious cases of emotional unresponsiveness, the child's emotional health may be in danger. Here we see the kind of avoidance behaviors described above—ignoring parental requests, turning away from parents, strong protests that appear inappropriate, or affect that is very concerning (e.g., emotional withdrawal, emotional dysregulation, frightened behavior).

To illustrate the adult-adult version of this language, consider the following situations.

Sara was having drinks with a few co-workers after work, and they were all talking about how they met their husbands. One friend, Lara, described that first meeting during a summer vacation and how for the past 15 years it has been bliss and that their love for each other has been overflowing. He then joined them for drinks! Lara continued the story and Adam seemed amused, but distant from it. She drew him in and worked to make him feel comfortable at the table and to make him feel good. Adam continued to seem pleased with the (over) attention and basked in it. But he also showed some incredulous body language, Sara thought, as if he may not have been perceiving the world in the same way as Lara, but she did not give the event much thought after that. They all later found out that he had been having affairs, and was about to move out. Lara was a psychologist and had no idea that there was anything remiss in the relationship!

Amelia, at 18 years of age, was looking forward to going to college, but also finding it difficult to physically separate from her boyfriend of three years. He was older and working in their hometown, and she had chosen to go away to a college, approximately three hours away. In the couple of months before going away to college, he began to seem a little less attentive or interested, but Amelia did not give these behaviors much thought, until she learned from a friend that he had started dating someone from his company. She realized that he may have interpreted her desire to go away to college as her "unresponsiveness" to him. She also realized that she had not read his own cues of "unresponsiveness" over time.

## 6a. Does This Dance Partner Involve You in His or Her Life?

## 6b. Do You Involve This Partner in Your Life?

Recall from the previous chapter that a healthy caregiver-child relationship has a balance between autonomous play and requests for adult involvement.

The child appears eager but not anxious to engage the adult. The relationship is a comfortable, positive one for both adult and child. At lower levels of involvement, children show more interest in the task at hand than in engaging adults' attention. It seems that these children are more oriented toward solitary play, with occasional reference to the significant attachment figures in their lives. Adults appear more like tools the children use when needed, rather than a desired audience. As the amount of involvement decreases, these children may avoid their significant caregivers altogether, literally turning their backs on them. Or the opposite may occur: the children may over-involve the caregivers, insisting they cannot play by themselves, offering toys, and constantly speaking to, looking at, or seeking physical contact from them. These actions may be accompanied by anxiety, whining, "acting out," complaining, and other forms of negative emotional expression. Such behaviors suggest that the children are assuming the lion's share of responsibility for maintaining contact and interaction with their caregivers.

Coming full circle to our roots in childhood, recognizing love language in early caregiver-child interactions, and translating it to peer-peer relationships or adult-adult relationships seems a natural progression in communication. The adult who engages and involves the other individual in his or her life is the adult who is being emotionally available.

> In an episode of "Sex and the City," one of the women "accidentally" runs into a man she has been dating, and he is with his mother. She has been wanting to meet his family, but he has not broached this type of topic. When he introduces them, the mother is polite and cordial, but has apparently never heard her name before.

> Cary, a divorced father with two children, one with disabilities and one normally developing, is dating a divorced mother, Tara, who has a 4-year-old daughter. They are like a blended family, basically living together, although they keep separate homes. He is involved with her life and her daughter and she is involved with his children and helps out the child with autism spectrum disorder, since she works in an organization utilizing Applied Behavior Analysis. Of note is that the father attends all school functions on his own and keeps that separate from his new relationship, which leaves Tara wondering about how emotionally available he is to her.

To summarize, try using the language of emotional availability not only with your baby, your child, or your adolescent, but also in the workplace and with your partner. In your adult-adult relationships, are you *sensitive* (reading others' verbal and nonverbal cues well)? Are you respectful of people's feelings and do you try to leave people with a good feeling?

---

**People remember not what you say but how you make them feel. Is your partner *sensitive with you*? Does your partner make you feel understood, or do you feel insecure about how he or she feels about you?**

---

Does your partner *structure* interactions and the relationship?

> **Does he or she support you in conversation, to find the right words and to support your way of life, goals, and dreams?**

Do you do the same for your partner in this relationship? Remember, it is all about relationships—how you are to your partner and how your partner is to you.

Ask yourself, is your partner *intrusive* and controlling and running your life? Or is your partner available for you without taking over?

> **In very close, committed relationships especially, there is a great deal of sharing, but does your partner take without giving or asking or is he or she careful about giving you space to grow and be or become your own person?**

Is your partner covertly or overtly hostile?

> **Are there frequent crises in your day-to-day life?**

Are you (or your partner) *responsive* to the other?

> **Is your partner happy and emotionally engaged with you when you are together, or does he or she seem detached, removed, or hard to reach?**

Very early in a relationship, it may be tough for some people to express themselves fully, but is your partner seeming to hold back intentionally or does he or she work at opening up to you emotionally? Is your partner *involving of you*?

> **Are you in this person's life or kept at a safe distance?**

These relationship check-up skills that we've covered related to emotional availability, as you can see, can help individuals form warm, satisfying, fulfilling, and emotionally available relationships in all areas of life if one allows this to happen.

> ### Developmental psychobiologists have shown that our brains and physiology seek out the familiar.

Audrey was a 55-year-old successful businesswoman in a relationship with a caring and emotionally available individual, Ali, a professor who was similarly successful. She had had a very difficult childhood, but "earned her security," having gone through years of therapy and a journey of her own. Although she enjoyed her nieces, she had no desire to give birth to or to adopt any children of her own. She had a very full life and felt she was generous and "giving" to relatives, friends, and co-workers in other ways. She had forgiven her own family for the pain she had to endure during the long journey to resolving her childhood sexual abuse. Although her relationship with her partner had lasted almost 20 years, she was beginning to feel that it was "missing something" and that she wanted "something undefinable." Ali, in contrast, cherished being available to the relationship, but felt that her availability was slipping away. Although she had earned her security and possessed a great deal of insight into herself and other relationships, additional therapy work revealed that a part of her may still be seeking the old familiar feeling of emotional unavailability she had known during her childhood, and that Ali's stable and constant emotional presence did not always seem familiar to Audrey.

As a 13-year-old, Jennie was not necessarily one of the popular girls at school, but she was as popular as she wanted to be. She had a small group of really nice friends, and the group included both boys and girls. They all met together in the same location every day at the cafeteria. As soon as they met, they would share items of food with each other, and they would take turns bringing the chocolate chip cookies or brownies. There was always something to share at this table! Jennie could also sense when things weren't going well in the group—people would start clamming up and there would not be much to talk about. But Jennie realized that that's the natural ebb and flow of relationships, and that when people seemed withdrawn, she or someone else, would start joking and, pretty soon, the ice would begin to thaw.

# Rating Your Relationship

For each of the dimensions of emotional availability (sensitivity, structuring, nonintrusiveness, nonhostility, responsiveness to the other, and involvement with the other), use the scales shown below to rate the quality of a "target" relationship. If you are a teen and reading this book, think of another teen, male or female, with whom you have a relationship as a close friend, school friend, ballet pal, soccer buddy, or other relationship. If you are an adult and are rating yourself, pick a specific adult with whom you are having a relationship (partner, spouse, elderly parent, family member older or younger than you), a specific adult with whom you had a relationship and the relationship ended, a specific co-worker or supervisor, or someone else.

If the scores on these scales are generally on the high end, it means that the relationship is making the individual feel *emotionally secure*. It does not mean that the relationship is "perfect," just that it has helped to create emotional security in the target individual (recall that you need to do the assessment for one individual in a relationship and then you can do the assessment for the second individual in the relationship, serially). The midrange indicates that there are clear inconsistencies, questions, and doubts about this relationship. Generally low scores suggest that the relationship is *insecure in a cool, detached, avoidant way*. The individual may be so emotionally shut down that true emotional connection is foreign territory or the individual may be moving away or keeping the relationship at a distant level, either intentionally for whatever reason or unintentionally. A cluster of very low ratings on some or many scales suggests that the relationship is *extremely problematic* and may even be traumatizing (e.g., characterized by violence or the threat of violence). A relationship may be very problematic due to one of the parties—both individuals' availabilities need not be problematic. Because a relationship is comprised of two individuals, being available to a relationship that has extremely problematic potential means that both have signed on.

Ratings hovering in the mid-range indicate inconsistent or apparent sensitivity. In the case of sensitivity, the adult is actually *apparently* sensitive but not really so (looks that way in many ways but is not creating a secure relationship), most likely because the adult is not authentic in affective exchanges. This individual may "look good" and do and say the right things, but there are "tell tale" signs of inauthentic expressions. It does not mean that this individual is a bad person (although it can!), but what it does mean is that the person may not know how to be authentic. The assessor could question whether manipulation is going on. Another type of apparent sensitivity is similar to what goes on in caregiver-child relationship—where the relationship is over-connected rather than secure and appropriately connected. This distinction is crucial: many over-connected relationships (which are not healthy) can look pleasant, but the over-connection undermines an individual's sense of growth and individuality. For example, in this type of relationship, the individual may be very demanding or subtly controlling the relationship.

Three different types of inconsistencies in interaction are often missed.

> ## Some interactions are viewed as highly sensitive when, in fact, they should be viewed as apparently sensitive, or the mid-range.

The first two types refer to inconsistencies inherent in the adult's behavior.

- The first type is the inconsistency between declarative knowledge and emotional/affective procedures. This inconsistency typically takes the form of the individual having enough knowledge about how to be sensitive that he or she can almost appear that way. At the declarative level, such an adult may try different things to keep the other's attention, may appear positively attentive, and often may be very accommodating. What belies this surface sensitivity is *affect*—which might be bland, flat, sugary sweet, pretentious, labile, anxious, hyperexaggerated, or hyperexcitable. Children and adults may show these strange or even bizarre qualities of affect. Affect is the key and, especially, whether the affect is genuine or feigned.

- Affective warmth is necessary for a high rating but it is not sufficient to get a high rating. An individual's warmth may be coupled with other qualities such as infantilization (i.e., treating the other as a child), or other subtle forms or strategies to control the other's behavior. These combined qualities of warmth with controlling, infantilizing, or other strategies may suggest either short-term or long-term relational issues.

- The third type of inconsistent sensitivity refers to inconsistency within the relationship. Because a highly sensitive individual has a keen sense of what optimal relationships *feel* like for the interactants, sustained unresponsiveness by the other would be emotionally received by the individual and alternative strategies would be pursued. *Thus, a highly sensitive individual would not engage in an interactional style that is one-sided.*

> These scales should be used when you have a chance to
> actually *observe* for about 20 to 30 minutes.

## Sensitivity[1]

5    *Highly sensitive.* Emotional communication between the equal partners, for the most part, is positive, appropriate, and creative. Each member of the interaction displays much *genuine*, *authentic*, and *congruent* interest and pleasure (as opposed to performing these behaviors).

3    *Inconsistently sensitive/ "apparently" sensitive.* The individual shows some signs of sensitivity, but some of it is pseudo-sensitivity, with feigned positive affect and/or other signs of not being genuine.

1    *Highly insensitive.* The individual displays few areas of strength in this relationship.

## Structuring

5    Optimal structuring: The individual lets the other lead while providing a supportive framework; that is, the individual offers the other the chance to explore and do things.

.

.

.

1    Nonoptimal structuring. The individual sets no boundaries for appropriate behavior in this relationship or the individual is neglecting and unavailable.

---

## Nonintrusiveness

5      *Nonintrusive.* The individual does not overpower the interactions, and allows the other to lead. Interactions are nonintrusive, smooth, and "spacious."

.

.

.

1      *Intrusive.* The individual is highly over-stimulating or bossy and does not leave enough space in the interaction for the other to explore and lead.

## Nonhostility

5      *Nonhostile.* There are no expressions of overt or covert hostility that can be discerned. The general emotional climate appears nonhostile.

.

.

.

1      *Markedly and overtly hostile.* This individual is overtly harsh, abrasive, and demeaning—facially and/or vocally. The individual's behavior is threatening and/or frightening.

## Responsiveness to the Other

5      *Optimal in responsiveness.* This individual shows an optimal balance between responsiveness to the other and autonomous activities; such behavior is combined with an affectively positive stance. This individual responds often to the other's bids, but without any sense of urgency or anxiety.

.

.

.

1      *Clearly nonoptimal in responsiveness.* The individual is unresponsive and detached from the other. Alternatively, the individual may be overly responsive.

## *Involvement with the Other*

5    *Optimal in involving behaviors.* The individual seems interested in engaging the other in interaction without compromising autonomous pursuits.

.

.

.

1    *Clearly nonoptimal in involving behaviors.* This individual usually does not involve the other in his or her life. Alternatively, the individual may over-involve.

# Emotional Availability Report[2]
# (for use when you don't have the opportunity to observe and are reflecting on a particular relationship between approximately equal partners, including child-child, teen-teen, and adult-adult relationships)

|  | Almost Never 1 | 2 | Sometimes 3 | 4 | Almost Always 5 |
|---|---|---|---|---|---|
| 1. This individual is upset a lot. | ☐ | ☐ | ☐ | ☐ | ☐ |
| 2. This individual doesn't talk to me much about what goes on in his/her life on a daily basis. | ☐ | ☐ | ☐ | ☐ | ☐ |
| 3. I wish this individual smiled more and seemed happier. | ☐ | ☐ | ☐ | ☐ | ☐ |
| 4. This individual listens to me when I talk to him (or her). | ☐ | ☐ | ☐ | ☐ | ☐ |
| 5. This individual seems genuinely happy when with me and with others. | ☐ | ☐ | ☐ | ☐ | ☐ |
| 6. This individual has lot of fun with me. | ☐ | ☐ | ☐ | ☐ | ☐ |
| 7. This individual has few friends. | ☐ | ☐ | ☐ | ☐ | ☐ |
| 8. This individual seems sad to me. | ☐ | ☐ | ☐ | ☐ | ☐ |
| 9. Others (e.g., teachers, my friends) have commented on this individual not seeming happy. | ☐ | ☐ | ☐ | ☐ | ☐ |
| 10. This individual and I do a lot together. | ☐ | ☐ | ☐ | ☐ | ☐ |
| 11. This individual listens to me when I disagree with him (or her). | ☐ | ☐ | ☐ | ☐ | ☐ |
| 12. This individual tries to talk to me when he (or she) has something on his (or her) mind. | ☐ | ☐ | ☐ | ☐ | ☐ |
| 13. When I try to talk to this individual about important matters, he (or she) seems disinterested. | ☐ | ☐ | ☐ | ☐ | ☐ |
| 14. This individual likes to be on his (or her) own and does not include me in important events or decisions. | ☐ | ☐ | ☐ | ☐ | ☐ |

| | Almost Never 1 | Sometimes 2 | 3 | 4 | Almost Always 5 |
|---|---|---|---|---|---|
| 15. I feel I don't have a lot of control, and this individual is the one with control around here. | ☐ | ☐ | ☐ | ☐ | ☐ |
| 16. I don't feel like I know this individual. | ☐ | ☐ | ☐ | ☐ | ☐ |
| 17. When this individual seems not to want to be with me, I feel hurt. | ☐ | ☐ | ☐ | ☐ | ☐ |
| 18. This individual gets angry easily and seems to get bent out of shape easily. | ☐ | ☐ | ☐ | ☐ | ☐ |
| 19. I listen to this individual when he (or she) tries to explain things to me. | ☐ | ☐ | ☐ | ☐ | ☐ |
| 20. I try to see things from this individual's perspective. | ☐ | ☐ | ☐ | ☐ | ☐ |
| 21. When things go wrong, I get angry and "bent out of shape" easily. | ☐ | ☐ | ☐ | ☐ | ☐ |
| 22. I am usually in a good mood around this individual. | ☐ | ☐ | ☐ | ☐ | ☐ |
| 23. When things go wrong, I tend to be flexible. | ☐ | ☐ | ☐ | ☐ | ☐ |
| 24. When I see that this individual isn't saying or doing something well, I jump in to correct him (or her). | ☐ | ☐ | ☐ | ☐ | ☐ |
| 25. It's difficult for me to separate from this individual and I always want to be with him (or her). | ☐ | ☐ | ☐ | ☐ | ☐ |
| 26. I shadow this individual's every step. | ☐ | ☐ | ☐ | ☐ | ☐ |
| 27. This individual seems to need a lot of assurances and reassurances of my caring and attention and seems to use distress to get attention. | ☐ | ☐ | ☐ | ☐ | ☐ |

## Scoring Your Test:

Questions #4, #5, #6, #10, #11, #12, #19, #20, #22, #23: If you answered 3, 4, or 5 on these questions, your EA is relatively high in this dance. Although individuals can have some low responses on these questions, if you received a total score greater than 33, you may be engaging in a relatively good level of emotional availability in this relationship.

Questions #1, #2, #3, #7, #8, #9, #13, #14, #15, #16, #17, #18, #21, #24, #25, #26, and #27: If you answered 1 or 2 for these questions, your EA with this individual is good. If you scored a total of 17-34 points on these questions, again, you are in a relatively good level of emotional availability with respect to this relationship.

# 5 The Spirit of Leadership

How can we apply the same principles of emotional availability to service through leadership? Essentially, the system used for parent-child relationships (where there are four qualities used to describe the adult and two qualities used to describe the child) can be used for equal-partner relationships as well as leadership. The difference is that all six dimensions of emotional availability are used for each member, so that sensitivity, structuring, nonintrusiveness, nonhostilty, responsiveness, and involvement are used for each participant in the relationship.

Parent-child—and in particular parent-infant—interactions are called "dances" due to the beautiful give and take that goes on in such communication. I have not used that term when discussing relationships with children in Chapter 2, however, mainly because I wanted to underscore the term "relationship," as children need to experience the important caregivers and adults in their lives as real, genuine, and long-lasting relationship or attachment figures. In Chapter 4, with respect to equal partners, I used the term "dance" to illustrate that often we are talking about interaction rather than relationship, and "dances" seem to capture the give-and-take of these interactions or communications, developed through the science of emotional availability. Here, in discussing leadership, I use the term "service," as we see an implication of appropriate wisdom, experience, and responsibility for the service role being described, although the leader is not necessarily older or wiser in the sense of comparison or superiority.

Let's think about each of the six questions before we get to the test, with respect to a specific leader's communication with a specific person or a specific group of people. Leaders not only have one-on-one communications, but also relate to a wide audience or group. In fact, "leader" is defined here as an individual in a position of authority who has one-on-one communications in the service role, and also relates to a group or different groups of individuals in this service capacity. Hence, within elementary, middle, and high schools, leaders include principals, assistant principals, and other administrators, but teachers most certainly also are leaders within their classrooms, as they relate to groups of children or youth. In institutions of higher education, administrators or directors who supervise and oversee the work of others and set a tone and direction to academic programs are considered leaders. Once again, faculty most assuredly are leaders in the context of their teaching or advising a group of students or in leading their research programs, which usually include teams.

Other leaders may include administrators of mental and/or physical health services, such as psychologists, psychiatrists, social workers, nurses, and pediatricians, among others, if they are in supervisory service roles and not only directly treat patients but also train and oversee the work of others. Still other leaders are in the field of law, and include, but are not limited to, attorneys and judges. These individuals are leaders because they have a "say-so" or authority related to the way children will be raised and how individuals will fare in the world. They typically have a short-term relationship with the people they serve, and often do not have the proximal contact that many leadership posts have, but they oversee and examine evidence (e.g., for children and families) that then lead individuals along specified pathways, such as how much parenting time an individual is allowed. Business leaders certainly also are key, including those who are heading small or large business concerns, and who have a role in how individuals fare in the world, either related to careers or financial futures (consider, for example, an investor for one's retirement account). Political leaders, both nationally and internationally, are also included here; leaders of countries most certainly relate to a wide audience, small groups, and even specific individuals.

Certainly, there is more to leadership than emotional availability—competence is a hoped-for quality by most constituents. But, beyond competence (competence in the subject matter is subsumed under the structuring dimension; see below), leaders need to be effective in communication. The "great communicator" is likely to be a good shepherd of the policies he or she sets forth in any setting. Further, the highest levels of competence are not inextricable from the person who has helped to create and execute them. The most brilliant ideas without the spirit (e.g., the ability and interest to be empathic and authentic, rather than apparently so) cannot lead to fully effective leadership. The "leakage" of negative or pseudo-positive emotional makeup can have dire consequences for the leader's service capability. It is no accident that the EA system developed for the parent-child relationship evolves into the realm of leadership, especially since a leader can often be seen as a parental/authority figure.

## 1a. How Sensitive Is the Leader in His (or Her) Service?

## 1b. Are Those the Leader Serves Sensitive with the Leader?

Consider the components of sensitivity taken specifically from Chapter 2.

- Predominantly positive, in terms of both facial and vocal expressiveness

- Appropriately responsive to the circumstances and the other's emotions

- Displaying congruence between verbal and nonverbal expression

- Accurately perceptive and appropriately responsive

- Aware of timing

- Flexible in terms of attention, behavior, and approach

- Showing acceptance of the other

- Empathic

- Able to handle conflict

Rather than taking these components of sensitivity one by one, as was done in Chapter 2, let us look at them in terms of how leaders provide a coherent whole, combining different elements.

The high end of this spectrum seems obvious—leaders who listen to, hear, empathize, and know how to handle or at least "ride" the tough times are viewed as sensitive, partly because they can read cues and respond appropriately to the cues. The key word is "understanding." At the high end, the leader understands his or her group and because of this understanding can respond in appropriate ways.

> Mr. Terry was the principal of a small middle school. He was very serious and, in some ways, distant from the children, parents, and (seemingly) the teachers. He would refer to every parent by last name and would expect the same for himself. Further, although he knew the names of all 200 children and all the parents, beginning with the first week of school, he rarely chatted at length with any of them outside of formal

appointments. Nonetheless, he was aware of how all the students were doing in school and was always available for meetings with parents. He seemed very present—during drop off, pick up, lunch time, and any special events. His steadfast presence created a sense of security for the children and, of course, the parents who entrusted their children to the school. When a parent talked with Mr. Terry about a student's uncharacteristically low performance on a science test, he replied, "I think what you are saying about a make-up exam makes sense, but, in all fairness to Mr. McDonald, we need to involve him in this discussion." Mr. Terry was an effective and emotionally available leader, not because he expressed an abundance of emotions, positive and/or negative, but because he was appropriate with his expressions for the context. As a leader of a school, his constituents were interested in whether he understood the children's needs, signals, and communications—that is, his sensitivity. Indeed, he was sensitive in interactions with the children when they talked to him and seemed aware of what they were trying to say or do. The children, in turn, seemed happy to be in the school, and students commented that he was "cool and knew where the students were at." Translated into the language of love, he "understood" them.

The low end of the spectrum also seems obvious, including those who are insensitive to the cues of others. At the low end, the leader may be completely oblivious to the reactions or cues from the group he or she serves. "Understanding" is not a priority.

Dr. Salsson, a tall man who typically sat with his long legs extended on an ottoman, was the chief psychiatrist at a major hospital in an urban area in Europe. At-risk mothers came to the facility with numerous problems in caring for their children. Although these women worked very hard to make improvements in their relationships with their children, Dr. Salsson rarely said anything complimentary about anyone's progress. In addition to verbally assaulting the women, he rarely noticed or reacted to the terror on the women's faces as they entered group therapy each week. One woman decided to point out to Dr. Salsson that his style was one that created fear for the women. His reply was that he could care less and that he was the one with the degree and license!

Often, leaders provide explanations for events based on a distorted view of reality (stemming from their own childhood histories; see Chapter 6 for a discussion of driving forces behind the language of emotional availability/unavailability). Although such individuals may be well liked to some extent, their rigidity and inability to hear more than a very narrow version of reality, in my view and as supported by empirical research on relationships, places them in the low end of sensitivity. They have trouble "understanding" the perspectives of others and, even though they may be nice and affable as people, as leaders they cannot move past their own (narcissistic) views of what is right and what is wrong.

Ms. McCanley was a national leader with whom people wanted to "go have some coffee"—she was likeable and comfortable with people (nice to talk with, a good sense of humor). She held strong beliefs and stood steadfastly by these beliefs. She was interested only in her own views and denied what she did not really want to see (as most people with substance abuse issues do). Rather than understanding the viewpoints of her constituents (the hallmark of a sensitive leader, who can "read" group cues and communications), she rigidly "stayed the course," stating that she was determined.

Let's attend now to an interesting aspect of human communication and the mixed messages that can be delivered, either consciously or unconsciously. That quality is "apparent sensitivity." It is up to the interactive partner to discern what is high in sensitivity and what is apparently sensitive, which is in the mid-range of the scale. For this, note that we need to attend to affect, empathy, and the congruence between different channels of communication, including verbal and nonverbal (tone of voice and body language).

---

**Apparent sensitivity is about being likeable and "looking good" without being genuine. As long as the interactive partner does not read these cues, the interactive partner, too, is less sensitive!**

As a leader of a major university, Dr. Yataf was bright, initially well-liked and well-respected, and seen as someone who would get a great deal accomplished during his tenure. He hired numerous well-known research-active faculty, increased the budget through fund-raising efforts and grant dollars, and created a climate of research productivity and teaching excellence. However, he had some interesting "emotional habits," such as being very nice in words but not delivering in deeds. This discrepancy between his words and his actions slowly began to erode the trust of his constituents. Morale was undermined, and many people became disenfranchised, even from this visionary leader.

Being truly sensitive refers to authentic expressions of affect and the genuine ability to connect with others. In fact, the ability to have a connection and to maintain it through trust is the hallmark of sensitivity. Moving goal posts, moving targets, the unaddressed, or the elephants in the room are the stuff of insensitive leaders of the twenty-first century, as they undermine the trust, confidence, or importance of those who are considered by virtue of rank to be "wise." But Dr. Yataf's apparent sensitivity was not catastrophic by any means, as he furthered the goal of a whole institution, sometimes choosing to overlook true human communication. The goals were nonetheless moral and ethical in the large sense of the advancement of science and humanities at a major university. Consider, in contrast, the more malicious variant of "apparent sensitivity" in the next story—that of domestic and international financial fraud.

Mr. Anthony was a well-respected and eloquent businessman, investing and making wealth for countless high- as well as middle-income individuals. His avuncular demeanor and wealth of knowledge disarmed those he had personally met, and his long-standing reputation as a brilliant investor created blind trust by those who knew him as well as those who only heard about him. He was the consummate apparently sensitive individual, creating an illustrious career based on this assumed quality of emotional availability, masking his emotional unavailability.

> Analyzing the messages from different channels of communication is key. Deception often "leaks" through nonverbal channels, but even more spectacularly through "countenance." It is nearly impossible for someone to live a lie and seem genuine. Looking at leaders to perceive their authenticity (versus deception, ranging from mildly deceptive to catastrophically deceptive) is not only an important skill of communication, it is essential to one's survival!

One of the best ways to assess whether a leader is sensitive to the individuals she or he serves is to see whether others are sensitive to the leader, as shown in the next vignette.

Ms. Phelps, the new Latin teacher at Keystone High School, was dynamic. Students rarely came to high school with any background in Latin. Yet, Ms. Phelps seemed to read the group so well that students remained with rapt attention throughout the class, and dropping Latin class was rare. She was exciting, even captivating, as a presenter. But more than that, she could also "read" her group of students so well that she knew when to have a pop quiz (to light a little fire) and when to have opportunities for extra credit (when the class was underperforming despite their best efforts). Her students were well-behaved and attentive in class. In addition to being dynamic, she was fair and just. She understood her students as well as how to deliver a difficult curriculum in the most effectively received way. When she fell short of the mark, her vast repertoire of teaching and communication skills made it possible to try alternative strategies to maintain interest. She was able to read *and* reach the students.

Whether the leader is reaching the constituents is very much assessed by the reaction of the constituents—a very simple but overlooked aspect of human communication. But, because it is so simple, leaders can assess themselves by such reactions, rather than feeling isolation and even helplessness. Certainly, many political leaders, especially those who assume leadership through nondemocratic processes, are not considering the reactions of others to their leadership. To them, leadership is a one-way street—the masses do not provide a good gauge of the effect of the leadership, as the masses have assumed a passive role and are not accustomed to being "read." They have turned off their signals!

## 2a. How Well Does the Leader Structure?

## 2b. Are Those the Leader Serves Structuring with the Leader?

Recall that structuring is about support, information, and vision:

- Verbal as well as nonverbal support

- Information and suggestions, without overguiding and infantalizing

- Vision

- Clear limits and boundaries, including moral boundaries

- Support that is welcomed

- Support, but not too much!

Leaders who feel they always need to be liked may have a difficult time with setting limits or making needed administrative decisions because they don't want to risk alienating others. A great way to set limits and to have those administrative iron-clad decisions is to first have an emotional connection, or "click," with the people who depend on that leadership. The more the leader knows, understands, and empathizes with the people he or she serves, the more likely that the structuring will be of just the right weight, rather than over-structuring with one's know-how or under-structuring.

Structuring occurs both verbally and nonverbally. In verbal ways, leaders provide information for children or others with whom they interact and work. In fact, providing information, knowledge, and perspective is a hallmark of leadership because in many ways a leader is assumed to have greater knowledge and, potentially, even wisdom. Further, nonverbal structuring (e.g., the subtle use of the gestural system) is important in all exchanges. Can the leader, during interaction, structure verbally and nonverbally so that others are guided and inspired, but not infantilized or over-guided and condescended? Can the leader provide critical pieces of information at points but still appear open to feedback? Or, does the leader rigidly follow his or her own dictates and knowledge and seem oblivious to or disinterested in constituent perspectives, with an "I know what is best" internal motto.

As was the case for sensitivity, structuring at its extremes, either positive or negative, is easily understood. Recall the case of Mr. Terry, the principal of a middle school:

> With teachers, Mr. Terry implemented videotaping policies to improve teacher quality, especially for new teachers, per standards for video-guided practice. When there was a dispute related to a grade, he supported the student in approaching the teacher to self-advocate. For both students and teachers, not only was there emotional support, but informational support—recall that structuring is the component of the language of love having to do with "competence" and "know how" related to the field at hand. Further, he also structured well with the parents. For example, he was known for his matter-of-fact expressions of violations, such as parking in the wrong place. Such violations, although rarely overlooked, were stated in a business-like, firm, but minimalist way, indicating his appropriate level of structuring for both children as well as parents.
>
> One morning, the parents received an email from Mr. Terry that a meth bust occurred in a neighborhood adjacent to the school and that the police had taken the relevant individuals into custody and had cordoned off the property. He informed the parents of the situation and offered the choice for parents to pick up their children, but stated that it was not his recommendation, given that the situation was under control. He further told them that he would be in contact immediately if the situation changed. Few parents in the school picked up their children early that day, likely because they trusted Mr. Terry's judgment and his word.

A very different, but nonetheless crucial, form of structuring occurred in our nation related to the 9/11 terrorist attacks. Quite simply put, national leaders were able to adequately protect the nation against terrorist attacks. To do so, they implemented a review of the Central Intelligence Agency, and improved national intelligence over time. This structuring (actually restructuring of the agency) and guidance was one piece of the mosaic that helped a whole nation remain safe from terrorism.

The next example illustrates the very skilled structuring of the current leader of the free world, who combines know-how with communication skills. Leaders cannot structure without information, knowledge, and judgment, lest they choose to rule without the benefit of wisdom. The Boulder, Colorado, newspaper, *The Daily Camera*, wrote in February 2009 under the headline "Obama structuring bailout":

> President Barack Obama promised on Saturday to lower
> mortgage costs, offer job-creating loans for small businesses,
> get credit flowing and rein in free-spending executives as he
> readies a new road map for spending billions from the second
> installment of the financial rescue plan. The White House is
> deciding how to structure the remaining half of the $700 bil-
> lion that Congress approved last year to save financial institu-
> tions and lenders. . . . He said his administration "will insist
> on unprecedented transparency, rigorous oversight and clear
> accountability so taxpayers know how their money is spent and
> whether it is achieving results."

Further, during the 2008 US presidential campaign, then-candidate Obama promised he would go "line by line" down the federal budget to understand and to eliminate any unnecessary expenditures. When this occurs, it would also be a positive example of leadership, illustrating structuring.

Conversely, when a leader makes good points but doesn't "take in" others' viewpoints, those others drop out emotionally, become disenfranchised, and may begin investing in leaders with viewpoints that match theirs. This suggests an inconsistency in the relationship of the leader with others. In other words, when a leader structures and guides without trying to take into account the constituents, or only seemingly taking their views into the decision matrix, the result is an "inconsistent structuring" because there is inconsistency between the leader and those he or she serves. The attempts to take others' viewpoints into account is essential—a leader cannot guarantee that others will want to be "rowing the boat" along with him or her. Regardless, attempts to include other views are of value in and of themselves and suggest a higher valence of structuring than would be the case without such genuine outreach. Such structuring efforts may be successful or effective with one group and less effective (or completely ineffective) with another group, depending on the emotional makeup of the different groups. Leadership can therefore be different in this aspect of emotional availability with different groups of constituents, but it always has the potential for movement and improvement, provided leaders can use the language of emotional availability in a conscious way. Assessing where one is at a particular point in time is the first step in being able to systematically make progress in the give-and-take of relationships!

The low end of structuring, that is, unstructuring, is also very important in terms of leadership.

> The director of an early childhood education school was brilliant, and opened up programming for senior citizens to come into the site and read to the preschoolers. He was praised by the students, teachers, and the community for this innovation. Yet, he had little idea of what actually went on in the program on a day-to-day basis. At the intellectual level, he was visionary in creating new programming; at the every-day level, however, he was unstructuring. In fact, one Thursday, the second floor (where the program was housed) was flooded due to a leak, but the director did not know about it until the following Wednesday, when he returned from a spontaneous vacation to the Alps. The school did not even have a phone number to reach him.

In contrast to Ms. Phelps, the Latin teacher described earlier in this chapter, consider the case of Ms. Johanssen, the French teacher at the same high school.

> Ms. Johanssen's classes were boring, and she rarely came to class with a lesson plan. Although the students craved structure, she remained "nice" but with too few rules and regulations (also known as structuring). Ms. Johanssen was very discouraged because the students were very disrespectful to her during class, talking out of turn, giggling, and throwing bottles into the garbage can as they left. She tried calling parents to seek out mental health services for some of the children, and when that did not receive much traction, she resorted to: "Stop doing that, Johnny. I will send you out of the class if you don't stop that." After having repeated these empty threats numerous times over the course of the semester, none of the students believed she was ever going to follow through. In addition, in an attempt to light a fire, Ms. Johanssen would say, "Enough of this nonsense, you will have an exam

tomorrow." The conscientous students would work all night to try to do well on an exam that was not announced well in advance, and the less conscientious would shrug it off. Invariably, the next day, Ms. Johanssen would announce that the exam was postponed until next week. The more conscientious students were always anxious about how to do well in the class, as there was no predictability, and the less conscientous students saw fifth period as a time to catch up on sleep.

The low end of structuring can also be important in nations, when leadership has not been appropriately structuring of groups or subgroups of individuals over which it has responsibility. For example, an unstructured system of investment banking contributed to the financial decline in the United States and the world, and many of us wonder whether deregulation was wise.

Another aspect of structuring occurs when the leader, by example, can illustrate appropriate structuring, and thereby role model this quality to the larger audience as part of the skill in emotional communication. Still another aspect of structuring occurs when the leader can support or encourage constituents in this quality, whatever the service endeavors undertaken by the constituents. For example, in a child care site, the director of the child care center can support the child care providers in learning effective structuring and in supporting them to continue using this skill. A principal can support the teacher(s) in using this skill by example (through incidental or observational learning) or by design (creating programming that supports the learning of this skill in classrooms).

> **The leader has the potential to create a "climate change" within the entity.**

The legal system can be observant of the all-important quality of structuring in parent-child interactions, not only when such situations are at the door of child protection services but in preventive contexts, such as when making decisions about child custody and access. They can try to learn about parental structuring (or differential structuring habits within the divorcing family), promote the importance of structuring for healthy child development, and realize its importance as a belief system in understanding the lives of children, adolescents, and families. After all, severely unstructuring parents are actually neglecting parents, who may not be aware of safety issues.

Thus, leaders have the potential to have great impact not only through their understanding, observing, and use of the language of emotional availability, but their ability to make decisions and provide support when deficits are noted. When unrecognized, deficits in the understanding and/or exercise of structuring can hamper the ability to be fully competent in one's role, regardless of the content area of the line of work, be it in business, education, law, or human resources.

In terms of the other side of the equation, are the constituents appropriately structuring? One form of appropriate structuring occurs when the "others" in the relationship support the leader, in words or deeds—and most clearly, if words and deeds match. But, it is difficult, if not impossible, for a leader to be optimally structuring if that leader does not have the support of others—be it an individual, a group, or different groups of constituents. When the other side of the equation is not participatory, structuring is likely to be of less use in a leadership context than when both sides are working together.

## 3a. Is the Leader Available without Being Intrusive?

## 3b. Are Those the Leader Serves Intrusive with the Leader?

Some of the qualities that are included in the view of nonintrusiveness include:

- Following the other's lead and not going beyond what the other "feels" is intrusive

- Not interrupting verbally

- Not constantly commanding, directing

- Not physically interfering, or manhandling, or using other physical gestures that are unwelcome

    Some reasons for difficulty with achieving nonintrusive leadership may be:

- An overdeveloped need to control the environment

- Viewing leadership as a one-way street

- Subtle or not-so-subtle personality dysfunctions (an adult with narcissistic tendencies—read "self-centered"—for example, might feel a sense of entitlement)

- Issues about control in the family who raised us

- Achievement, overachievement, or an exaggerated need to prove something

- Being too available

- Caring too much!

Optimal nonintrusiveness is an important aspect of the universal language of love and it is in this way that the individual gives space to others—space to "return the serve." Many people can feel a sense of narcissism, which gives them the entitlement to control conversation and to control decisions. Often, but not always, the reasons for intrusiveness can be benign, such as caring too much for the other individual or for organizational goals. But intrusiveness also is about control and a conviction (even if not conscious) that the leader's own views are the most important and those of the constituents are less important to the whole picture.

It is important to remember that intrusiveness is determined not solely by one adult's actions, but also by others' emotional responses. For example, in the area of parent-child relationships, what is nonintrusive at one age point (e.g., spoon-feeding a baby) is considered intrusive at a later age point (e.g., spoon-feeding one's 14-year-old, which I witnessed as a clinician!), and part of the reason for the sense of intrusiveness is the partner's reactions (the 14-year-old kept moving his face away from the mother but the mother felt he needed to eat some more).

In some ways, however, intrusive alliances can sometimes lead to passivity and a lack of will in the partners. In that case, further intrusions are not necessarily met with resistance. In fact, totalitarian regimes are known for the (often) passivity and sense of futility of the populace, at least for some periods of time. Decisions are made for the individuals, who digest them without any chewing. One sure thing in our democratic society is that the debates among political parties and the media's heated coverage helps us all, by limiting intrusive leadership.

One might think that leadership that is high as well as low on this dimension would be obvious to most of us. The first of the following vignettes is about an optimal scenario, and the second about making an extreme decision, without "hearing" the important role of the universal language of love in the lives of our children and families.

In the world of child care sites, especially for infants and toddlers, much work and planning typically goes on to take care of the children. Tara was a new child care professional, did not have children of her own, and was not feeling confident about her abilities and training (she had a bachelor's degree in English). Her supervisor, Albertha, realized that confidence was likely to be a big issue for Tara in learning the trade. She visited Tara's room frequently, as she did with all the other rooms, and would point out when Tara did something wonderful with the children. At first, Tara felt that she rarely did anything well, even changing a diaper! But, as Albertha saw the good in her actions and behaviors with the children, Tara began to do more of these actions. Albertha's nonintrusive guidance was inspirational.

A judge listens and watches carefully as the mother, Elena, describes the minimal involvement of her ex-partner with their baby, Nadia. Elena also describes that she would like to move back from the United States to Argentina with Nadia, to be closer to her family. She also explains that her ex has become very involved and wants to prove himself worthy of sensitive fathering. The judge also hears evidence from expert witnesses of the importance of fathering and of difficulties Elena has had in creating a secure attachment with her baby. For example, her baby, now 18 months old, routinely goes and hugs her father when they are reunited, and her father returns the hugs and kisses, but he then follows Nadia's leads and interests in the world rather than forcing his agenda upon her. As further described in the (observational) custody evaluation, Elena often interrupts Nadia's play, wanting a hug and kiss and not knowing when to stop asking for more, and even demands kisses as Nadia is absorbed in fantasy play with her little dolls. The judge listens, says little, and then makes a decision that Nadia will go to Argentina with Elena, as children belong with their mothers, and that her father is too busy as an emergency room physician to have time for her anyway. His decision (as a leader working with and responsible for the welfare of children and families!) does not seem to take into account that Elena is intrusive and that Nadia may benefit (in the sense of secure attachment) from her father's more sensitive and less intrusive style.

Also at an extreme is the following scenario, in which leaders decide for their constituents the most private and sacred aspects of their lives—that involving their children.

A national leader feels that he knows what is best for all women and children and thus views a ban on abortion as crucial. The right of a woman to choose is not seen to be as important as the right of the leader to choose in the best interests of the unborn child. Similarly, others believe in a "nanny state," which dictates that somehow the government needs to attend to the welfare of all children. Where stem cell research is viewed as unethical, the state becomes "intrusive" into the lives and decisions of scientists.

Between these extremes, is the "benign" intrusiveness of leadership, with micromanagement of day-to-day operations, which often puts a damper on the mental space of constituents, and can also create passivity and a look to the leadership for a "nod" on most issues, even if trivial. Such benign intrusiveness may be quite consciously viewed as being for the common good, but at the unconscious level, it shows the lack of confidence in the constituents. Like a well-meaning, authoritarian and (over) protective mother who reminds her child, "Do you have your hat and mittens?" and "Have you had enough to eat?" just one time too many, the leader with good intentions would do well to step back and look at the big picture of others with leadership roles within the entity, and delegate responsibility and have confidence that constituents, too, can make good and independent decisions.

Just as I described both sensitivity and structuring in "relational" terms or in the terminology of a "dance," again, intrusiveness can be seen as not just a one-way street, but as something that is noted in the context of a dance. Surely, if the partners are able to take cues from each other about the next step (although it may be so natural, and therefore, imperceptible to the observers), they are not being intrusive with one another if their dance is smooth and one partner does not step on the other's foot. Such is the case also with nonintrusiveness in service—a leader is available, but nonintrusive to the extent that he or she does not go faster than the constituents, like a runaway train. But even more important than speed is how the speed is " received" by the constituents. One constituent may think that corporate reorganization is just what is needed for productivity, whereas another loses sleep because the change may seem threatening.

What is also important is that the constituents not be intrusive into the space of the leader. This is an oft-missed point. After all, a leader has authority for independent decision making. The capacity to maintain appropriate boundaries and to be wary of boundary dissolution is key to keeping intrusiveness at bay, from both sides of the equation.

## 4a. Does the Leader Show Any Overt or Covert Hostility?

## 4b. Do Those the Leader Serves Show Overt or Covert Hostility?

One cannot be viewed by others as emotionally available—that is, high in EA—through attacks, whether overt or covert. Rather, the relational know-how that gets others to attend is nonhostility—*even* in the context of stress and *especially* in the context of stress.

> When Walter Mondale suggested that Reagan was too old to be president, rather than attacking his opponent, Reagan commented that he would not even think about his opponent's youth and inexperience.

> During the campaign, we saw Barack Obama staying with the issues and having a light and refined touch. What was striking to many was his gentlemanly demeanor, and how he stayed the course with such good manners, despite much poking to "lose his cool."

In the relationship of leaders with their constituents, what is most concerning is, of course, the other extreme, that of the perpetration of violence, especially against one's own people. Violence is the endpoint of expressions of hostility. Leaders can victimize their own people, including women and children, or subgroups of their own people, based on religious or ethnic membership. Alternatively, leaders can choose to enable by remaining passive (like the bystander) to violence that is being inflicted on individuals in society. The potential for violence potential is certainly at the extreme of overt hostility. Past behavior is the best indicator of future behavior! A history of lack of empathy toward life (be it a child, adult, or animal, or in thoughts about living things) is a good predictor of lack of empathy in the future.

> **Whether violence is inflicted directly or indirectly, the possibility of abuse (physical or verbal) can be at its worst when the leadership has this potential.**

Recall the vignette at the beginning of this chapter concerning Dr. Salsson in the hospital setting for at-risk mothers.

> Marjo was a 25-year-old, attractive ex-con and ex-drug addict. At a group therapy session, Dr. Salsson verbally attacked Marjo and called her a "good for nothing," saying, "When will you see yourself for who you are?" The good doctor then moved to the next client, Mira, saying, "I don't believe a word you're saying. What is in that mind of yours, anything?" During the 50 minutes of the group session, the captive audience of this leader was scared and wondering who would next be verbally assaulted. Both Marjo and Mira left treatment prematurely.
>
> Dr. Salsson described his program as full of women who needed boundaries and who needed to be "called on" about how bad they were. He was providing this boundary and a mirror, in his view. Dr. Salsson himself had come from a history of physical abuse in his family of origin, and had seen this experience as a "character building" time in his life. He had no patience for weakness, and in his view, these women were weak. He had recreated an abusive context in his leadership role. The executive director of the larger hospital organization had hired Dr. Salsson, but with no check on his view or philosophy of relationships, merely his degrees from prestigious schools and his active license with no reported problems.

These leadership oversights have tremendous impact on the lives of individuals. Often, leaders can distort reality (based on their own childhood histories; see Chapter 6 on the driving force behind the language of emotional availability). Needless to say, the women coming to this setting to recover from violent relationships during their childhoods and in their current relationships were not leaving better able to handle life, but potentially even worse, as the leaders did not have a clue about *genuinely* emotionally available relationships.

The interesting mid-range of the continuum of nonhostility/overt hostility is that of covert hostility, or "leakage." Leaks refer to irritations, frustrations, teasing, and the like. Dr. Salsson was overtly hostile as he verbally assaulted some of the women at the hospital's group therapy session, but even before the overt signs, his demeanor was covertly hostile (e.g., joking with the women in a condescending way).

Leaders have a special role to play in the regulation of negative emotions in their organizations. The child care director who sees a child care provider sighing in frustration, mostly bored, or huffing and puffing when doing the tasks of caring for babies (all signs of "leakage" or negative emotionality), or ignoring or delaying responsiveness to children who are crying or hitting others (also signs of hostility because background negativity is just as difficult for individuals as direct negativity) must act. By example or by design, an effective leader can support the regulation of negative emotions in the entity and begin to build an emotionally availability community!

Once again, we return to the "relational" or "two-way street" quality of the language of emotional availability. Just as leaders may be overtly or covertly hostile, but also part of the solution in creating emotionally available environments and communities, leaders may also be on the receiving end of potential nonhostility/covert hostility/overt hostility. How does the leader relate to those who are in some way hostile? Can the leader help titrate hostility that is directed at him or her?

Indeed, the regulation of covert and overt hostility for the group(s) one leads is perhaps one of the most challenging aspects of leadership, particularly when the overt and covert hostility brews within a subgroup. These relationships must all be handled so as to evoke at least respectful responses, if not love. Let it be said that the power of "emotional presence" is in communication. Even without something specifically being said or something specifically being done, leaders can communicate in the face of others' aggressive impulses. That is to say, a powerful emotional presence, without saying or doing something specific, is strong communication in and of itself, and is often palpable in effective leadership.

## 5a. Is the Leader Emotionally Responsive to Those He or She Serves?

## 5b. Are Those the Leader Serves Emotionally Responsive to the Leader?

Just as in the caregiver-child relationship, the only way to tell if a relationship is working well is to look at the other individual. Important in terms of leadership is the parent-child analogy, with the leader in some way usually having skills at a level that is higher—or at the very least, authority that is higher than that of the individuals. Is the leader responsive to the initiations of the others (their suggestions, inputs, or even shows of positive affect and support) or is the leader unaware or even rejecting? Furthermore, are others responsive to the leader as a very good index of how the leader is doing on the job?

An aspect of others that indicates lack of optimal responsiveness is what we call a "negative cycle of connectedness." The others may be negative or otherwise "act out" in myriad ways as part of being in this relationship. Not only is such behavior not optimal responsiveness, it is negative responsiveness.

These clues are likewise important for leaders who work with children (e.g., child care directors, attorneys, judges) as they observe and interact with children or see others interacting with children. The more emotionally available the child, the more we can conclude that the adult interactants, be it parents or nonparental caregivers, also have been emotionally available to this particular child. In contrast, a child's emotional unavailability to the adult is a very profound indicator of a problem in the relationship—emotional availability is a relationship quality, not an inborn temperament characteristic. Thus, an "active" and deep understanding of what it means for the other to be responsive is an important part of a leader's tool kit of communication.

In the case of national leadership, often our leaders are surrounded by "yes" men and women. Such may also be the case with leaders in other contexts, even leaders who work with children. Yet, by tone or deed, one can still detect the emotional responsiveness or lack of responsiveness of others. When people are less interested in listening to one's views, less likely to be emotionally positive around that person, and less likely to want to support that person's views and actions, then responsiveness is faltering.

Although highly responsive and highly unresponsive actions can be palpable to most leaders, the middle ground of beginning to lose that palpable responsiveness can also be sensed by good leaders. When constituents need to become intrusive and hostile to be heard by the leader, tension is the result.

> A once-popular international leader began to lose the support and responsiveness of her constituents as the public began to disagree over her foreign policies, insistence on war as a means toward peace, and economic deregulation. After many years, not only the constituents but also other leaders, including those from her party, began to distance themselves from her, with "yes" men and women being replaced by emotionally and even physically distant men and women. She remained steadfast in her views, however, choosing not to see the unresponsiveness of the constituents and connected with a small remaining group of loyalists.

Moving from the constituents' side of the equation to the leader's side of the equation, let's look at the level of responsiveness of a leader. Responsive leaders are those who take into account the viewpoints of others, rather than being "shut down," where leader and constituents are like "ships in the night." A leader who is emotionally shut down remains detached and out of touch. It is not difficult to imagine such a leader—one who remains only in the office and rarely ventures into the office corridors, lest he or she run into a constituent and might need to chitchat.

> Mrs. Kapany was a middle-school social studies teacher who believed that middle-school children should not be given chances to retake any exams or to have any extra credit. "This is middle school," she used to say, suggesting the expectation of a high level of excellence, with no excuses! When Ana approached her about feeling sick on the day of the last test, for which she received a D, Mrs. Kapany was not responsive to the student's overtures about a make-up exam, and said, "You will take this as a lesson about life." Despite insistence by both Ana and her father, Mrs. Kapany remained steadfast and said she would not administer a make-up exam, even after Ana's diagnosis of salmonella.
>
> In this case, Mrs. Kapany offered a "good" reason for her

unresponsiveness—students need to be excellent, and accepting excuses means that students are not learning to be strict on themselves. Hence, Mrs. Kapany was trying to teach important life lessons, but this important lesson was out of context, given this particular student's health situation. Mrs. Kapany had a change of heart and mind, however, and called up Ana's parents, saying, "I thought about this situation, and while it is completely against my teaching philosophy, I am willing to give a makeup to Ana because her performance on the last test was so discrepant from her prior performance and because of her health situation." The important life lesson learned by Ana was that individuals in leadership roles (especially educators) can choose a more relationally available response, and this allowed Ana to advocate for herself in future school-related scenarios. Because she was "heard" in this situation, she began to think that others in authority positions also would hear her, if needed.

The mid-range is sometimes the most interesting of the emotional availability/emotional unavailability phenomenon. What about those who are too connected and therefore too responsive, especially given the leadership status of the individual and the boundaries that need to be set for that status?

Dr. Liber was a professor of education at Central Community College, and passionate as a teacher in the classroom and as a supervisor of student teaching. Students came to work with her because of her national reputation in the area of children with disabilities. She was so popular, in fact, that she and her students had dinner together several nights a week and she was quick to eradicate any negative evaluation of any of her students. They knew she could be trusted to "stand up for them," and she most certainly did—sometimes to the point of verbally attacking other faculty members if they dared to give negative feedback to a student teacher during the annual evaluations. Dr. Maya, Dr. Samuels, and Dr. Lehigh all agreed wholeheartedly with Dr. Liber on all occasions, and nipped any criticism (even if realistic or well meaning) about the students or themselves. Trust outside the close-knit network of faculty and students was a rare commodity. Although she was emotionally responsive, in the view of many, Dr. Liber had created an enmeshed (over-connected) network of relationships at work that had blurred the boundaries of their roles and clarity of perception. She and the other faculty were leaders and had lost objectivity with respect to each other as well as the students. But, because both faculty and students received many "emotional supplies" from well-intentioned Dr. Liber, they did not realize that she was actually hurting their professional development.

Role confusion and boundary dissolution can be important aspects of the language of emotional availability/unavailability because they can create diffuse boundaries and overly emotional exchanges, which ultimately are not healthy in leadership roles. Appropriate boundaries, not detached and not over-connected, can be how individuals can discern others' responsiveness to them and their own level of responsiveness to others. Being responsive is not the goal—having a healthy level of responsiveness is what the language of love is about. One can actually hurt others by caring at inappropriate levels.

Magistrate Connelly was initially impressed with Jessica John's relationship with her young daughters, 3-year-old Talia and 4-year-old Iana. In the midst of a violent relationship with her spouse, Jessica had maintained a close relationship with Talia and Iana, and had apparently protected them from being physically abused. Her spouse, suffering from bipolar disorder as well as the recent loss of his livelihood as a construction worker, frequently became agitated, tense, and irrational. During those episodes, he seemed to pick a fight and someone or something had to take the brunt of his rage. In the month since he lost his job, Jessica had to make two trips to the nearby hospital's emergency room for treatment of her bruises and lacerations. The children seemed anxious, but so responsive to their mother that Magistrate Connelly did not initially sense any issues related to the children's well being. The girls were always smiling and giggling (albeit in a nervous and anxious way) and would try to make their mother laugh, especially to cheer her up. They were also constantly clinging to her, and would not want to even go to the bathroom without their mother. Over-responsiveness, rather than an appropriate level of responsiveness, was seen, and as a leader working with children and families, it was important for the magistrate to understand the phenomenon. These children were overly empathic. As a leader, the magistrate was able to first notice and then to suggest professional help for Jessica, Talia, and Iana to work on their overly responsive relationships.

# 6a. Is This Leader Involving of Other(s)?
# 6b. Do Others Involve the Leader?

Recognizing the similarity of love language in early caregiver-child interactions, and translating it to leadership roles is a natural progression in the understanding of communication. The link with one's early childhood also is clear from research, and will be described in Chapter 6. The leader who engages and involves other individuals likely is one who was engaged by others in his or her own family of origin.

To summarize, consider the language of emotional availability not only with a baby, child, or adolescent, but also in the workplace and in different roles in life. A leader who engaged and involved was exemplified by then-candidate Obama, who mobilized unprecedented numbers of young and first-time voters to begin thinking seriously about the political process and their need to question the status quo. First, he involved a volunteer pool and then the volunteer pool reached out to other voters. As president, Obama's outreach and involvement efforts to other leaders across the aisle is already palpable, even in the midst of serious thought about the multiple crises facing the nation.

Institutional leaders also need to observe whether they are being involved and engaged by their constituents because constituents who are feeling that they are making a connection will engage and involve and in positive more than in negative ways, and involving is better than those who have given up on their leaders!

> By the end of his time as director for national atmospheric research, George Anton's constituents were no longer emotionally and positively involving of him, professionally or personally. After mismanagement of numerous government contracts awarded to his unit and "borrowing" money from one of the contracts, he was a disgraced leader. The emotional communication of unavailability was palpable, and one of the tell-tale

signs was that others were no longer involving and engaging him in their projects and rarely solicited his views.

# The Spirit of Leadership: An Interventionist or Therapist as a "Leader"

In addition to relating to a group, leaders also relate to some individuals in a one-on-one fashion, and this may be at a deep and therapeutic level. Here we discuss the case of a particular type of leader—that of an interventionist or therapist. When we speak of an interventionist, particularly an early interventionist, we need to think about how that individual supports and moves a relationship to higher levels. In the case of any type of intervention work, the interventionist is successful to the extent that a supportive and emotionally corrective relationship is established. For example, the emotional availability of an interventionist is thought to further and enhance the emotional availability of the parent/family in relation to a child. By working to create an emotionally available relationship with the caregiver, the interventionist provides a corrective emotional experience for the adult, who then can be an emotionally available figure for the child. In this example of early intervention, the leader is working one-on-one with a parent or family, but, what about other potentially therapeutic contexts?

What about the emotional availability of a therapist in the context of psychotherapy with a child or adult. Here, the work to be done is not through a caregiver, but in direct work with the client. The emotional availability of the therapist is thought to help the client in exploring new ways of looking at the past as well as new ways of looking at the future.

In fact, Robert Emde, M.D., has done some excellent reflection and writing on this topic, that is, on the emotional availability in the context of therapy or intervention. He emphasizes how an interventionist (or therapist) becomes emotionally available in relation to the relationship. The influence of relationships on relationships is important, both for the interventionist working to enhance caregiver-child interactions and the therapist in so-called individual psychotherapies, where the professional uses the therapeutic/intervention relationship to influence a network of other relationships in the client's wider world.

From my vantage point, the emotional availability test can be applied to both the interventionist and the therapist and may be a guide to those in training. For example, is it feasible that professionals in training may first appear "apparently sensitive," but as training progresses, they may learn to work on this quality and become more genuinely and optimally sensitive. Emotional availability testing can be an important part of furthering the quality of the corrective emotional availability that is deemed necessary for change. Once again, the tests in this book are for "personal" use, and should not be used in any professional context. Please write to www.emotionalavailability.com for more information on this concept and the professional versions of these tests.

## Rating Leadership

For each of the dimensions of emotional availability (sensitivity, structuring, nonintrusiveness, nonhostility, responsiveness, and involvement) shown below, rate the quality of a "target" relationship. The target relationship may be between the leader and other(s). Observing refers to your filming or directly observing for 20-30 minutes (by taking notes) that particular relationship, and than deciding which rating best described the target relationship.

If the scores on these scales are generally on the high end (7, 6, and to a lesser extent 5), it means that the leader is being received well. The midrange indicates that there are clear inconsistencies, questions, and doubts about this leader: in the case of sensitivity, the adult is actually *apparently* sensitive but not really so (seems likeable, but may not be trustworthy or may be connected to others in an unhealthy way, with diffuse role boundaries). This distinction is crucial: many over-connected relations can look pleasant, but over-connection is not healthy. Generally low (but not the lowest, that is, 2.5/3.0) scores suggest that the leader is received as *cool and detached*. A cluster of very low ratings on some or many scales suggests that the leader is *extremely problematic* and may have had a traumatized past. After the leader is rated, then rate the "other" or the "others" as a group.

> These scales should be used when you have a chance to actually *observe* for about 20 to 30 minutes.

## Sensitivity

5    *Highly sensitive.* Emotional communication, for the most part, is positive, appropriate, and creative. The individual displays much genuine, authentic, and congruent interest and pleasure (as opposed to performing these behaviors). Positivity is seen, even in the context of "tough love."

3    *"Apparently" sensitive.* The individual is pseudo-sensitive, with feigned positive affect and/or other signs of not being genuine.

1    *Highly insensitive.* The individual displays few areas of strength in this domain.

## Structuring

5    *Optimal structuring.* The individual shows an appropriate degree of structuring. The individual's bids are successful in structuring interaction, and the individual is consistently good at structuring.

     .

     .

     .

1    *Nonoptimal structuring.* The individual sets no boundaries for appropriate conduct and provides too much freedom without rules or expectations.

## Nonintrusiveness

5    *Nonintrusive.* Interactions are nonintrusive, smooth, and "spacious." In interaction, the individual is available to the other as a support without being intrusive and has a quality of emotionally "being there."

     .

     .

     .

1    *Intrusive.* The individual is highly directive and controlling and may be abusive.

## *Nonhostility*

5       *Nonhostile.* There are no expressions of overt or covert hostility toward the other that can be discerned by an observer. The general emotional climate appears nonhostile.

.

.

.

1       *Markedly and overtly hostile.* This individual is overtly harsh, abrasive, and demeaning—facially and/or vocally. The individual's behavior is threatening and/or frightening. Threats of separation or threats of violent behaviors are seen.

## *Responsiveness to the Other*

5       *Optimal in responsiveness.* This individual shows an optimal balance between responsiveness to the other and space; such behavior is combined with an affectively positive stance. This individual responds often to the other's bids, but without a sense of urgency, anxiety, or affect that is inappropriate to the context.

.

.

.

1       *Clearly nonoptimal in responsiveness.* The individual rarely shows emotional and behavioral responsiveness (of the optimal kind) when engaged with the other and rarely responds to the other's initiative. This individual is unresponsive and detached from the other. Alternatively, this individual is overly responsive and potentially needy.

## *Involvement with the Other*

5       *Optimal in involving behaviors.* The individual seems interested in engaging the other in interaction and doing outreach, without compromising his or her individuality and individual goals.

.

.

.

1      *Clearly nonoptimal in involving behaviors.* This individual usually
       does not involve the other. Alternatively, this individual is
       overly involving of others, sometimes through distress.

# Emotional Availability Report[1]
## (for use when you don't have the opportunity to observe and are reflecting on a particular relationship in the context of leadership)

| | Almost Never | Sometimes | | | Almost Always |
|---|:---:|:---:|:---:|:---:|:---:|
| | 1 | 2 | 3 | 4 | 5 |
| 1. This individual is upset a lot. | ☐ | ☐ | ☐ | ☐ | ☐ |
| 2. This individual doesn't talk to others much about what goes on in his/her daily life. | ☐ | ☐ | ☐ | ☐ | ☐ |
| 3. This individual doesn't seem happy. | ☐ | ☐ | ☐ | ☐ | ☐ |
| 4. This individual listens to others when talking with them. | ☐ | ☐ | ☐ | ☐ | ☐ |
| 5. This individual seems happy when with others. | ☐ | ☐ | ☐ | ☐ | ☐ |
| 6. This individual relates well with others. | ☐ | ☐ | ☐ | ☐ | ☐ |
| 7. This individual has few good confidantes. | ☐ | ☐ | ☐ | ☐ | ☐ |
| 8. This individual seems sad and/or angry. | ☐ | ☐ | ☐ | ☐ | ☐ |
| 9. Others have commented on this individual not seeming happy. | ☐ | ☐ | ☐ | ☐ | ☐ |
| 10. This individual interacts sufficiently with others. | ☐ | ☐ | ☐ | ☐ | ☐ |
| 11. This individual listens to others when they disagree with him (or her). | ☐ | ☐ | ☐ | ☐ | ☐ |
| 12. This individual tries to talk to others and include their viewpoints. | ☐ | ☐ | ☐ | ☐ | ☐ |
| 13. When others try to talk to this individual, he (or she) seems disinterested or detached. | ☐ | ☐ | ☐ | ☐ | ☐ |
| 14. This individual tends to decide things on his (or her) own, without much consultation or interaction. | ☐ | ☐ | ☐ | ☐ | ☐ |
| 15. This individual doesn't have a lot of control, and others try to take over. | ☐ | ☐ | ☐ | ☐ | ☐ |
| 16. It's hard to understand this individual and his (or her) motives and ideas. | ☐ | ☐ | ☐ | ☐ | ☐ |

---

[1]Copyright ©2009 by Zeynep Biringen, Ph.D. All rights reserved, including translations, any adaptations, and derivative works. May not be reproduced in any form without written consent of Biringen, per international copyright laws. For more information on the full version, to be used for professional work in this area, please visit www.emotionalavailability.com. The versions presented here were developed for this book and are not research-based. They should be used only for personal reasons, and never for professional evaluations.

|  | Almost Never | | Sometimes | | Almost Always |
|---|---|---|---|---|---|
|  | 1 | 2 | 3 | 4 | 5 |
| 17. This individual has very strong reactions when others don't do what he (or she) wants. | ☐ | ☐ | ☐ | ☐ | ☐ |
| 18. This individual gets angry easily and seems to get "bent out of shape" easily. | ☐ | ☐ | ☐ | ☐ | ☐ |
| 19. Others listen to this individual when he (or she) tries to explain things. | ☐ | ☐ | ☐ | ☐ | ☐ |
| 20. This individual genuinely tries to see things from the perspective of others and values open communication. | ☐ | ☐ | ☐ | ☐ | ☐ |
| 21. This individual gets angry and resistant when things go wrong or when others disagree with his (or her) viewpoints. | ☐ | ☐ | ☐ | ☐ | ☐ |
| 22. This individual is usually in a good mood, or at least is even keeled. | ☐ | ☐ | ☐ | ☐ | ☐ |
| 23. When things go wrong, people tend to be flexible rather than angry with this individual. | ☐ | ☐ | ☐ | ☐ | ☐ |
| 24. Others try to control or overcontrol this individual, and try to intrude into his (or her) "space." | ☐ | ☐ | ☐ | ☐ | ☐ |
| 25. It's difficult for this individual to separate his (or her) views from those of others. | ☐ | ☐ | ☐ | ☐ | ☐ |
| 26. It's difficult for this individual to have viewpoints independent from those of others. | ☐ | ☐ | ☐ | ☐ | ☐ |
| 27. This individual seems to need a lot of assurances and reassurances from others and seems to use distress to get attention. | ☐ | ☐ | ☐ | ☐ | ☐ |

## Scoring Your Test:

Questions #4, #5, #6, #10, #11, #12, #19, #20, #22, #23: If you answered 3, 4, or 5 on these questions, your EA is relatively high. Although individuals can have some low responses on these questions, if you received a total score greater than 33, you are engaging in a relatively good level of emotional availability.

Questions #1, #2, #3, #7, #8, #9, #13, #14, #15, #16, #17, #18, #21, #24, #25, #26, and #27: If you answered 1 or 2 for these questions, your EA is good. If you scored a total of 16-32 points on these questions, again, you are showing a relatively good level of emotional availability.

# 6 Emotional Availability/Unavailability, Childhood History, and Perceptions

## Family History

People bring all kinds of personal history into their relationships, and that is not a problem. The problem arises when those issues are left unresolved. As adults, our own parents are often our only models of how to relate to children as well as how to relate to others, so they usually have a powerful influence on us, no matter whether we want to emulate them or be completely different. As adults, we need to recognize the heritage we have brought with us from the family in which we ourselves were raised, and to replicate what was good and try to eliminate what was not.

Social scientists Carol George, Nancy Kaplan, and Mary Main at the University of California, Berkeley, developed a state-of-the art interview to assess individuals' family-of-origin experiences (called the Adult Attachment Interview). The interview is very detailed and enables the interviewer to obtain information about the individual's experiences during childhood. It also does something quite tricky—it can help us understand beyond the childhood experiences of individuals by going beyond the surface of what they report. In other words, we gain information on both what they say happened as well as some things they may not consciously remember. Our relationship skills have a great deal to do with our family history—not just what we consciously remember, but, more likely, all of the largely unconscious learning that we bring to our relationships.

## Security during Adulthood

### The "Raised Secure" Individual

Many (fortunate) adults recall having positive experiences as they were growing up, and these individuals are likely to continue that positive

127

heritage in their own personal relationships, with their children, in their marriages, and with other relationships. Research has shown conclusively that intergenerational transmission of the language of love is a fact. In other words, if you remember that you were accepted and your parents were warm and kind to you, then you are likely to be more emotionally available for the next generation, as well as in your wider relationships. Individuals who were raised secure usually provide a coherent account of what happened in their childhood, with minimal real inconsistencies in their story lines. For example, if a mother describes her childhood as beautiful and her own parents as loving and caring, we would expect to hear clear examples of many loving connections during motherhood, such as this mother planning for a Valentine's Day party at school and utterly delighting in her own child's (as well as other children's) pleasure at the party.

I have now used the Adult Attachment interview with hundreds of mothers and fathers. Many clear and detailed examples of loving years are typically provided, with the individuals having access to a relatively full range of emotions. Other assessments exist to tap into memories of childhood relationships, and they, too, provide a link with how people relate to others—for example, the relationship one individual has with another in the context of being a couple or being in a marriage.

Most individuals who recall positive and happy relationships during their childhoods *really* had such relationships, and their children, if they have children, benefit from such a past. If they do not have children, they may have important relationships with other children through the work that they do, in child care, as attorneys or judges, as caseworkers, or in extended families or social networks. There are few people who do not have some contact with children, be it personally or professionally.

- Such individuals are not recalling idealized versions of their childhoods; they were truly happy during their childhoods.

- Many such individuals have very easy access to their emotions. They smile easily, joke easily, and they are not overly guarded with their emotions. They can relate.

- These individuals are likely to have marriages and/or relationships that are more open and communicative, where there is a "click" or connection, mutual topics, and ongoing regard for each other.

- Most important, those who are "raised secure" have been found to be more sensitive, appropriately structuring, nonintrusive, and nonhostile in their relationships with their children, and their children are more responsive and involving of them! These are the six elements of the universal language of love!

> Twenty-six-year-old Gloria, a teacher and writer, remembered her late mother, Sarah, as a single mom with an abundance of love and care. She remembered her mother as saying that becoming a mother was very important to her and, although she had no family nearby, she decided to adopt Gloria through an open adoption process, even though she knew that the 17-year-old biological mother had been using alcohol during her pregnancy. Although she remembered early problems with acting out, she also remembered how she thrived in the stable life provided by Sarah, who taught piano to children in her home so that Gloria could be with her during those early years. It was a good feeling remembering that Sarah's piano students always delighted in seeing her and playing with her each week. Between sessions, Sarah or another parent would make sure to read to Gloria. In fact, Gloria remembered growing up in a loving *community*, where she felt special and sought after by all of the students and their parents every day. When she was an adult, Gloria recalled her childhood as a happy one, and easily remembered all the fun and joy she shared with her mom and the piano community.

## The "Earned Secure" Individual

Many individuals in the "earned secure" classification relate well to their children, although they may be more guarded with their emotions than the "raised secure" parents because they have had obstacles to cross on the path to their security. They have passed insecure terrain and are now in secure territory, at least within themselves. Many, however, describe horrific experiences. Does this mean that they are not good relationship material? What we find is that some individuals, either through their own psychotherapy, through help from a supportive person such as a spouse, or through other life experiences, have come to reflect on their early experiences—sometimes experiences as severe as abuse—and have come to rework those experiences. They have gone on a journey!

Reworking is a difficult process and does not happen overnight. We find that when individuals have become reflective about their family-of-origin experiences, their new way of thinking can transform their relationship not only with their own children but also their relationships in general.

> These "earned secure" individuals have created their own sense of understanding of what happened, and in many cases they have forgiven their parents for the stresses of their childhood.

These individuals are resilient, but not through "steeling" or "shutting off" emotions; they have coped with the emotions available to them. Because they have not tucked their emotions into a compartment as they coped with the stress of not having emotional needs met, they can now have access to those feelings as they relate to others.

This process entails open, coherent, and reflective thinking. The permission to reflect on the past without immediate threat of trauma or terror (although the actual events may have been painful) allows these individuals to live on a plane where emotions are permissible in relationships. As parents, these individuals raise the next generation in an emotionally available way. Because they are aware of the negatives in the past and have "unshackled" themselves from those negative effects, they have gained a freedom that they share with others in their lives.

This holds much optimism for the future!

> As individuals give themselves permission to examine the past, they become freed from repeating it. Their interactions with their children, their spouses or partners, and their friends are generally sensitive and caring, and rarely intrusive and hostile. In return, their children, partners, friends, and so on are generally responsive to them and involve them in their lives.

A hopeful and optimistic view is that individuals can earn their security in adulthood—they are not constrained by their pasts if they don't want to be. To earn security during adulthood, you need to:

- Have access to childhood experiences, and then you can work on such memories. Professional help may be needed if you have struggled with traumatic early experiences, as "access" can be quite partial.

- Be aware that such realization and work takes time and reflectiveness.

- Know that not everyone chooses to do this work—in fact, it is not clear what makes people want to change. But you are clearly in emotionally healthy company if you choose to earn security.

- Again, most important, remember that the "earned secure" also speak the language of love with their children, just as well as those who were "raised secure"!

> When interviewed about his childhood relationships, President Barack Obama remembers loving grandparents and a loving mother, but an absent father. He also surmises that he may have been affected by his mother's physical absence during a part of his childhood, although they remained emotionally connected. Just like many of the "earned secure," a journey is needed to come to terms with many of the issues left by an emotional vacuum. He did take that journey, through writing of his memoirs and with the establishment of many positive relationships over the years. As we know, he enjoys positive and loving relationships with his children, with his wife, and, if watching him campaign was very much a view into the language of love, with a whole nation. He often ended his speeches with "I love you" or "I love you back."

As the psychologist who developed the assessment method for understanding emotional availability in relationships and as a researcher in this area and in the adjacent area of emotional attachments during childhood, I have been an observer of leaders as they come and go. Our most recent research project, which was on "leadership development," was presented to leaders in the community to provide them with attachment-relevant information.

> **It is my belief that "earned secure" individuals present tremendous leadership potential—mainly due to the cognitive and affective ability they have gained during the process of overcoming the conflict of their childhoods.**

The ability to resolve conflict within their own deepest paths can lead individuals toward the ability to resolve conflicts, unlike the "dismissing" individual (described below) who denies the existence of conflict.

## *Dismissing Individual*

A subset of adults (about 20 percent of the normal population) who recall positive experiences with their own parents actually "idealize" their family-of-origin situation. They project a positive image of themselves and of the adults who were a part of their childhood. Because memories of their childhood are too painful, they distort what transpired in their family of origin into a more consciously acceptable form. The process is unconscious; such adults rarely realize that what they remember isn't accurate. Indeed, many of these individuals have difficulty remembering their childhood at all. It is as if certain aspects of childhood are blocked. When these adults are interviewed about their childhood, they provide less "meat" and far fewer details than the secure individuals we just discussed. Often they are not very expressive and generally dismiss the importance or expression of emotions. Do you have any dismissing individuals in your life?

When asked the importance of early childhood experiences for later personality development, these adults are puzzled by the question and say that they don't see a link.

> One such father, Kevin, told me, "My mother, didn't have much of an effect on me. I don't see any link. I'm my own person; I really don't have much to do with her." Kevin was almost compulsively self-reliant as an adult, yet he could make no connection between his almost compulsive self-reliance and his emotionally rejecting mother.
>
> A woman, Pauline, said, "My mother was the best mother possible and everyone on the block loved her." Her mother kept a great house and always had wonderful presents under the Christmas tree. As an unimportant afterthought, Pauline added, "She gave great parties, especially birthday parties for the three boys in the family, but she never had one planned for me. . . . She was a wonderful hostess at the parties. She was a lovely woman and I miss her." Pauline couldn't appreciate the lack of coherence in her own description of such positive, even idyllic family-of-origin descriptions, and the fact that she herself never was the recipient of one of these wonderful parties. She had idealized her description of her own mother and completely ignored any specific details that could not be incorporated into the larger picture of her mother as "wonderful."

Pauline was unaware that she had had a negative early experience with her own mother. Her idealized description of her childhood was actually the evidence of a negative past.

Sadly, individuals who have little access to their emotional lives most likely will go about their lives in an emotionally vacant way.

> **They are so dismissive of the value of relationships and of emotions as part of important relationships that it is easy for them to be good providers or good at keeping the house clean or good at some other functional aspect of relationships that is praised in our society. But what they lack is the ability to be part of the give and take of emotions!**

If they have their own biological or adoptive children, they may interact in a cool and distant way toward them. If they are foster parents, they may remain emotionally uninvested. Such behavior does not mean that they love or care any less; it merely is difficult for them to interact in a loving way or to demonstrate their love. Instead, many such parents do nice things for their children and take care of other (nonemotional) more functional aspects of life. Their children are rarely happy and responsive. Many of these caregiver-child interactions are like "ships passing in the night" as each goes about his or her own routines. They are not emotionally sensitive to their children, and their children grow with emotional disconnects from the parents.

Many of these individuals have marriages that work and relationships that work, in the sense of continuity. However, there may not be the openness of communication or mutuality of emotional communication in these relationships. They are more likely to dismiss affect or emotional issues in favor of goals and goal orientedness or task orientedness in the marriage. As long as both partners do not invest in open emotional communication, the unions can work—until one begins to become earned secure, of course.

While the intergenerational cycle of abuse (the experience of abuse being repeated across generations) within families is important enough for us to pause, the intergenerational cycle of abuse within nations and across nations is also important enough for us to consider!

## Individuals Who Are Preoccupied or Over-Connected to the Past

A small group of individuals are the opposite of the dismissing individuals—they are actually very emotional. I don't mean this as a "healthy" option, however. Just because individuals are emotional does not mean that they can nurture healthy emotional connections.

In fact, over-emotionality is what is described here. Many of these parents are either very angry or anxious/distressed about the past and what they did not receive during their childhoods. They have access to their emotions (unlike the dismissing parents), but are "stuck" in the past and have not been able to resolve the problems so that they can now have a coherent view of the present and of the family of origin as fitting into their sense of self. Forgiveness is not there!

Such individuals interact often in a warm way with their children. Sometimes it is difficult to see at first glance that there is anything remiss in these relationships because the adults are likable—but often they are intrusive, not observing boundaries between themselves and others; or they are inconsistently sensitive, quite warm and nice at times, and then they "fly off the handle" at other times, not being able to regulate their emotions. It is difficult for their children to feel genuine emotional connection with them due to their inconsistent behavior.

Further, many of these individuals have issues with separation, and see that as a threat to connectedness. They therefore respond to separations (e.g., leaving a child in day care) with intense anxiety and transmit such uneasiness to the child. Not having experienced clear boundaries between family members, in behaviors and/or feelings, such parents have trouble separating themselves and their needs from those of their children.

> Relatedness through over-connection is what we see in these relationships. Do you know anyone who may be over-connected to their families through anger and anxiety/distress and continues that style with their adult-adult relationships, co-workers, and friends?

One mother, Jayne, a teacher and artist, whom we had classified as preoccupied or over-connected, described a story that showed she could not make important connections about her past. She first started describing an incredibly fun childhood with great vacations in the outdoors. Jayne described great parents who took pride in each of the children. She also described incredible closeness among all family members. She said that the parents gave each of the children many reasons to feel special, and were wonderful with each of them. But, as Jayne continued to recount her past, she began to cry more and more uncontrollably, with the recognition (on her own) that there was no reason to cry about some of what she was describing (for example, how great the vacations were). Jayne, in fact, used up half a box of tissues, continuing to wonder why she was so emotional. She then went on to describe a volcano of angry emotions about her mother, who did not live up to her promise of being caring in some ways and that Jayne felt alone as she made many life choices. She wondered why her parents never gave her their approval with respect to her career as a dancer, her boyfriends, her choice of life partner, and her husband's career. She then described a physician brother, Keith, who was in jail for committing a murder borne of road rage, again without a pause in the recounting of the perfect family. Jayne continued without pause to other topics about her family, not even stopping to provide any detail or to make any connections between Keith and any aspect of their family life. Jayne did not recognize that her over-connected demeanor with her own child was born of her feelings about her own upbringing by parents she viewed as emotionally detached and judgmental.

## *Disorganized Individuals or Those Unresolved About Loss(es)*

A last pattern observed in our studies involves individuals who experienced an unresolved loss or a traumatizing event at some point during their childhood (perhaps by death, divorce, or sexual abuse) or during their adulthood (again perhaps by death, divorce, sexual assault or rape; giving birth to a child with disabilities; experiencing prenatal, perinatal, or infant losses, such as miscarriage, stillbirth, or Sudden Infant Death Syndrome; or the death of an older or adult child).

> **What is important here is not so much that there was a loss as that the individual has not "worked on" and resolved issues related to this loss.**

An individual with a child who has a severe illness or disability might need to go through a period of mourning the "loss of the perfect child." Only after some time and processing of what this loss means can the individual (and the couple) open new avenues of understanding and expression. Studies indicate that when parents have worked on and resolved such loss issues with respect to their children with disabilities, they are likely to have secure babies and children. The loss of a child by death is considered one of the most difficult grief and loss issues for an individual and for a family.

> One of our research participants had lost two children to still-birth after going through full labor with each of them. A heavy smoker, she blamed herself for these deaths (smoking has been linked with stillbirth) and experienced much anguish during this time. When we later saw her, with her 5-year-old son, she seemed very emotionally disconnected both from her son and from others. In the interview, she talked about her other children as if they were still alive.

> Another mother, who had experienced a stillbirth one year before, gave birth to a beautiful, healthy daughter. Yet, because she had not "worked on" on her previous loss (and losses are not only death-related, but also include all the omissions of understanding and compassion from our own parents), when her daughter was born, she became disorganized in her thinking and psychologically and emotionally abandoned him and the family, recreating the trauma of the prior loss in the new situation. The couple soon divorced.

> Ashram is a 13-year old boy in a Middle-Eastern country ravaged by war. His father and mother have been killed and he is now an orphan taking care of his younger siblings. Many of his family members also have been killed and all the children have seen violence around them for most of their childhoods. Will they be able to earn their security and help their countries and themselves as they grow up, or will they be angry and hostile? Can they be sensitive to the needs of others? Can they grow to speak the universal language of love?

## A Negative History

Approximately 20 to 30 percent of individuals consciously report that they have had negative early experiences with their family of origin. I'm referring to serious deficiencies in child rearing. Some adults report they were physically or emotionally abused, and others describe milder issues of rejection or lack of understanding by parents. Certainly actual cases of physical, emotional, mental, or sexual abuse are readily identified as negative experiences. But sometimes even cool rejection or omissions in empathy are enough to create negative early experiences for a child. For example, I have interviewed many parents who stated that they were never held or hugged in times of distress. Such omissions of empathic understanding can be as serious (if not more serious) for a child's emotional development as obvious physical punishment.

If childhood experiences have been negative (e.g., abuse), individuals need to work at many different levels. For example, if parents were abused as children, they may vow not to abuse in their own family. But they may still engage in subtle putdowns and less obvious signs of bullying with their children or with their spouses or even at work. It is as if these individuals were able to eliminate obvious methods of abuse but couldn't avoid the more subtle kinds of abusive interactions they probably learned in the family of origin.

For those with negative childhood experiences, working on one's psychological and relationship issues provides a positive "break" or discontinuity between childhood and the present. Such work must inevitably include accessing and reworking one's emotions. Some of the biggest problems in parent-child and adult-child relationships arise when individuals refuse to access their own emotions because they wish to avoid the pain of doing so.

> Such individuals—who have had abusive relationships in their families of origin, for instance—might think, "You grow stronger with experiences like that but you shouldn't dwell on the bad things in your life. You're weak if you stay at that level. You have to be strong and not let yourself get weak and full of feelings." One individual, who had lost her father at the age of five, said in a defiant tone, "Sad—no I was not sad. I was happy about it, because after he died, we had a much better life, and better material possessions because all the uncles chipped in." She was not only cool and detached in her role as mother but also in her role as wife.

For people with early negative experiences, feelings are something to be avoided, dismissed, and even disposed of. They then enter their own parent-child relationships with a "stiff upper lip" and dismiss the importance of emotions in their children's lives. One such parent said, "No need to go to the hospital, right, Olivia? You're not brain damaged, are you?" when her daughter bumped her head on a nearby coffee table as she was crawling about. Such parents deny to themselves and their children the importance of emotional connection or emotional availability. Instead, they rely on what I call "functional availability." They take care of the things that are needed to keep the family running, but they never share their feelings with their children or ask to share their children's feelings in return.

> One such individual, Sarah, devoted many hours at her son's school helping the children learn to weave. The many artistic creations in her son's school were truly beautiful. Yet along with that great "function," this mother rarely offered any emotional response to her son, Paul. During one of our sessions, Paul hurt himself with a toy sword as he played with toy knights and princesses. As Paul began to cry uncontrollably, Sarah watched coolly, as if responsiveness was not part of her repertoire. In fact, she continued to read the book she had brought into the session; she barely blinked. Finally, the observer went into the room and offered some words of reassurance to Paul, and he was then able to calm down and continue with the rest of the session.

"Functional availability" is characterized by parents doing everything for their children's basic care and survival and very little for meeting their emotional needs. The meeting of functional needs is good *providing*, but meeting a child's emotional needs as well is good *parenting*.

# Making Connections between the Past and Present

Professional help is likely to be most helpful in freeing an individual from a negative past so that his or her children are freed from its intergenerational effects. Many individuals have difficulty accessing the past, and some dialogue on how the connections can be made is likely to be in order.

This is also true of leaders who work with children and leaders who need relationship skills (*all* leaders in the twenty-first century need relationship know-how). If a leader who works with children is dismissing in his or her family history, then he or she may be so with observing others' interactions with children as well. He or she may not understand the importance of emotional connection due to the lack of familiarity with it. Similarly, a national leader who is dismissing may be perceived by the public as cool, distant, aloof, and not able to connect with others on a one-on-one basis. This leader may be astute on the issues and may be able to "sell" on the basis of experience, but what is needed in the twenty-first century of complex relationships in the world and a global context for relationships is the ability to be flexible in relationships. The role of communication is key! Good leaders are flexible, not rigid and blocked off to a portion of their existence—that of emotions and communication. Everything is not competence and experience. Leadership involves people and people respond to the emotional, not just tasks and machinations and mechanical/automated prose.

Worse than leaders who are dismissing are those who are traumatized leaders. If a leader has had significant demons, such as alcoholism, abuse in one's family of origin, either in the past or present, and has not worked actively and consciously to resolve these issues, then we have a traumatized individual as a leader. This is the plight of many leaders in our global society. A whole field of psychohistory would indicate that these leaders will make decisions that impact society in terrorizing and traumatizing ways. Traumatized children usually become traumatized adults, who may then go on to relate to others in these ill-fated ways. We can only surmise about the types of leaders in the next generation, if we do not provide critical emotional communication skills to the next generation of leaders, worldwide, hopefully while they are still young!

# Recommended Reading[1]

Bluestein, J. (2001). *Creating emotionally safe schools.* Deerfield Beach, FL: Health Communications, Inc.

Brooks, R., & Goldstein, S. (2001). *Raising resilient children.* New York: Contemporary Books.

Cytryn, L., & McKnew, D. (1996). *Growing up sad.* New York: W.W. Norton & Company.

Faber, A., & Mazlish, E. *How to talk so kids will listen and listen so kids will talk.* New York: Rawson, Wade Publishers, Inc.

Goleman, D. (1995). *Emotional intelligence: Why it can matter more than IQ.* New York: Bantam Books.

Gottman, J. (1997). *Raising an emotionally intelligent child.* New York: Simon & Schuster.

Hendrix, H., & Hunt, H. (1997). *Giving the love that heals: A guide for parents.* New York: Pocket Books.

Middleton-Moz, J., & Zawadski, M. L. (2002). *Bullies: From the playground to the boardroom.* Deerfield Beach, FL: Health Communications, Inc.

Rubin, K. H. (2002). *The friendship factor: Helping our children navigate their social world—and why it matters for their success and happiness.* New York: Viking.

Seligman, M.E.P. (1995). *The optimistic child.* Boston: Houghton Mifflin Co.

Stepp, L.S. (2000). *Our last best shot: Guiding our children through early adolescence.* New York: Riverhead Books.

Tofler, I., & T.F. Di Geronimo (2000). *Keeping your kids out front without kicking them from behind: How to nurture high-achieving athletes, scholars, and performing artists.* San Francisco: Jossey Bass.

---

[1]www.emotionalavailability.com provides a list of scientific readings on emotional availability.

Lightning Source UK Ltd.
Milton Keynes UK
11 April 2011
170739UK00001B/9/P